A LIFE WINDING DOWN

What I have learned, but I could be wrong

By

Barbara Kemm-Highton

Copyright© 2018 Barbara Kemm-Highton

ISBN: 978-1-62249-217-6

**Published by
Biblio Publishing
Columbus, Ohio
BiblioPublishing.com**

TOPICS

Introduction	1
I: Mediums, UFOs, the Paranormal, and 2012	3
II: Marriage	9
III: Spirituality	13
IV: Death	19
V: Politics	25
VI: Aging	29
VII: Raising Children	33
VIII: Happiness	39
IX: Health	43
X: War	51
XI: Education	55
XII: Ego	61
XIII: Addiction	65
XIV: Evil	69
XV: Animals	77
XVI: Media and Entertainment	79
XVII: Angels	83
XVIII: Sexual Assault and Harassment	87
XIX: Earth	91
XX: "America Land of the Free"	97
Poem	106
Epilogue	107
Suggested Reading and Other Resources	109

Barbara Kemm-Highton

Dedication

To my husband who patiently listened to all of this. You are always my support and I thank you.

To my sons. You were the reason I wanted to do more and better.

To my beautiful, smart granddaughters. Always know that I am here for you in this life or the next. Love to all my family and pets here on Earth and those beyond.

It is the energy that never dies.

INTRODUCTION

I am barreling through what is often called "the golden years," or less euphemistically "senior discount days." I woke up one day and said to myself (old people are known to talk to themselves), "I should write a book about life and what I have learned." I wanted to leave my sons something else to contemplate about the path their lives might take. My granddaughters, hopefully, will skip some of the roads I decided to travel that were just basically stupid. My husband "gets me" as far as he can but prefers ESPN.

This is not my first foray into writing. I was an English teacher, although I have misspelled a few words (to my own horror), and I used the term "irregardless" until just recently when someone finally told me it wasn't a word.

I wrote two books about true crimes, *A Body on the Farm: The Disappearance and Murder of Carol Blades* and *Missing or Murdered in Missouri: Unsolved and Solved Cases*. My inexperience was terrifying, but I was most proud of the fact that I helped those families to keep their stories alive. So, here I am after saying I never wanted to write another book, doing it again. I was a closet author from the time I was a child, and a lot of what I wrote even baffled me. Where did this come from? I will give you a sample poem later and you, too, may scratch your head.

Someday I hope all of my family reads this when they get their first hint that it is time to figure out who they really are and where they might end up when "the final curtain comes down," or at least maybe when the first application for an AARP card comes in the mail—provided we still *receive* mail old-school.

For any "senior" (which used to be a prestigious moniker when we were in high school) reading this, I hope

Barbara Kemm-Highton

that I haven't led you astray with all of my scattered knowledge.

Oprah, if you happen to read this (Ha!) don't worry that I will try to mentor others to help them become more enlightened; I am still a little concerned that I might be wrong. Oh, and I do have some very stubborn beliefs that I refuse to let go of. That being said, they are my opinions only. Feel free to scoff, or if I have already "passed on" contact me on the Other Side to tell me if I was right about anything.

I will be serious about some subjects because time is frankly running out and irreverent about others because they are amusing to a point. Topics are in no particular order of importance and I will also try to use as many clichés as I can to reference the "end of days."

My only hope is that you can relate to the journey.

No pessimist ever discovered the secret of the stars or sailed an uncharted land or opened a new doorway for the human spirit.

Helen Keller

MEDIUMS, THE PARANORMAL, UFOS AND 2012

I am fascinated by these people who can talk to the spirit world or channel, or anything related to ghosts or UFOs. I started with Edgar Cayce, who can be a little difficult to read at times, but I collected most of his books. If you haven't read anything about him, start with *There is a River* by Thomas Sugrue. Then I worked my way through Sylvia Brown, John Edward, James Van Praagh, Alison Dubois, Shirley MacLaine, George Anderson, Ruth Montgomery, Rosemary Altea, and Sonja Choquette, and I became friends with a woman who is also a psychic detective, Judy Price. I cannot prove to you or anyone else that what they do is real, and when they get it wrong or make a mistake, I am left with a few doubts myself, but I also realize that they are not super-human. I strongly suggest you read *The Afterlife Experiments* if you are confused about their gifts. Many of them performed very well in cold readings in a clinical setting.

These are the few eerie or "twilight zone" moments in my own life.

1. I had an imaginary friend. I know that one can be explained away. However, some mediums have another explanation. Children appear to be fine-tuned to the spirit world (until adults mess with their energy and tell them that it is their imagination) when

Barbara Kemm-Highton

they may actually be visiting with their spirit guides or guardian angels or ascended beings.

2. I knew my high school boyfriend was killed in a car accident before anyone told me. I cannot readily explain this.

3. As a child, I was obsessed with horses. My father was a talented graphic artist and I begged regularly for copies of his horse head sketches. We lived inside the Springfield, Missouri city limits, but that did not quell my incessant begging for a horse of my own. There is a puzzle made from a photo of me on a horse that I recently discovered and it still is a prized possession. In my quest to know if I had lived before, I had a past life reading and was told that I was a male horse trainer for Attila the Hun. Hmm. It is a part of early nomad history that his horses were considered monstrous and mysterious; their breed was rumored to be mythical due to their girth and fierceness. A decidedly deadly army of expert archers in great numbers on menacing, muscular steeds must have panicked many villagers in the Roman Empire, but the folklore concerning the discovery of the bones of a super-sized animal have not been proven, so far. Also, my name is just a little too close to "barbarian" for comfort.

4. I saw a creature one night when I was about 16, a human-like monster on a bicycle when I was in a car with three other teens. No, I wasn't drinking that night. It was not a mask, but its whole appearance seemed, well, otherworldly. I have never talked to the others in the car about it, but many years later I was watching a documentary about the strange sightings in Point Pleasant, West Virginia recounted by two young couples. While they were driving past an old abandoned TNT plant, they claimed they were being chased by what appeared to be a moth-like man. This

A Life Winding Down

account and several more spawned both a book and a movie. Needless to say, I could relate.

5. I have had moments when I thought a sense of dread kept me from being harmed. It felt like a literal gut punch. I know you and the skeptics might be calling this a gut feeling based on healthy fear. (Keep in mind healthy fear wasn't exactly in my vocabulary for a lot of high school and most of college. Oblivious was a little more accurate).

6. I saw a huge silver metal door/window in the sky when I was traveling down a county road in the Ozarks on a sunny, very cloudless, day. This one made me question my own sanity, but I saw what I saw even when it should not have been there. I have no plausible answer, but this door was massive and it blinked in and out in the clear blue sky in just seconds. Later, I read a very strange book about all the space ships that are pretty much parked out there monitoring the earth and its particularly destructive inhabitants. We have the potential to affect the entire universe with our nuclear powers, after all. It was comforting to me and brings whole new meaning to the well-worn phrase, "We are not alone." And they might have some mammoth transportation based on what I saw.

7. When my mother passed away, I was walking into the kitchen of my home with all that grief sitting right there on my chest squeezing my heart. I was having trouble breathing, when suddenly I was filled with warmth beginning from my toes and then winding through my body. I clearly heard her voice in my head say, "I am okay." I can hear the rebuttals in my head as well, "hot flashes," "overcome with grief," or a personal favorite, "hallucinating." Hey, I don't know either, but I felt much better. I choose to believe it was my Mom. It sure sounded like her.

Barbara Kemm-Highton

8. When my beloved basset hound, Drooper, died, I came home just 30 minutes after he was "put to sleep" and saw an image of him in the kitchen where he always stood. I know. I know. The grieving thing again. Others will say he left his energy behind. I miss him.
9. I have known for a number of years now that I have some sort of unseen guides named Mary and Jasmine. If I concentrate, I see Mary as a small, curly headed woman who is both old and young at the same time. I get the sense that she is my grandmother "Mayme" (Mary Margaret). The other is very exotic and middle-eastern looking. (I always think of the song "Walk Like an Egyptian"). I asked about my personal guardian angel and Ariel was the name I was given. Oddly enough, I happened to stumble upon a small book of astrological signs connecting angels to our birth sign and, lo and behold, Leo is connected to the angel Ariel. Hmm. I am clueless about his appearance, only that "it" appears to be a "he" and looks pretty much the way angels might look, but not like John Travolta with those big cumbersome wings in the 1996 movie *Michael*. Ariel is wingless. Actually, I believe the spirits and angels (or alien beings) are androgynous, but they come to us in familiar forms of gender (instead of one-eyed, ten-fingered, hermaphrodites that might scare us off). Wait! Maybe some do. You can stop rolling your eyes now. I am finished, unless something else comes along at the "final hour." (I like that term even less).

I would like to see a ghost. Well, maybe not one of those skin-scratching kind like they have in some houses and lots of ghost hunting shows, but just a tragic looking woman in a period piece dress. Truthfully, it would scare the crap out of me. (Is it just me, or are all of the ghost hunting shows

A Life Winding Down

normalizing this occupation so much that most of us are okay with "things that go bump in the night" as long as it is on reality TV?)

Next up, UFOs. They are everywhere. I want to know who is on board and if they are appalled at what they are seeing here (if not, they should be since we are essentially dragging our knuckles along the ground and still killing each other like mindless robots—I will get to War later). And don't get me started on crop circles. Have you seen some of these amazing pieces of art that pop up all over the world literally overnight. Google them. Be in awe and stop believing the skeptics that drunken farmers in pubs or savvy science students are doing all of them. No way they can show up like they do and alter the very ground. A leading expert in the study of these phenomena has determined that a large percentage of them are man-made, however, he has no clue who is making them or why and roughly 20% seem to be from some other more complex source. Wake up people. There are many, many, many witnesses and documents, videos, strange sightings, weird occurrences, abductions, and paranormal experiences out there. Aren't you even a little bit interested?

If this is not enough for you still, Google any temple in Mexico or Egypt or Peru. There are cities and monoliths all over the globe that baffle even the engineers who study them. Case in point, many obelisks in the ancient world have very precise carvings that are geometrically perfect, intricate and detailed. Then Google the crude tools dated to that era and try to imagine a perfect angle made with a stone tied to a stick! Some engineers have said that only lasers and machines could be responsible for their accurate carvings.

By the way, the Bible and other sacred religious texts that we believe in as gospel are rife with paranormal activity: parting the Red Sea, rounding up two of every animal on earth, raising the dead, talking to angels with wings, virgin births, turning a few loaves of bread and fish into enough to

Barbara Kemm-Highton

feed thousands, hands on healings etc., etc. and we do not blink an eye. Why are UFOs, Near Death Experiences, ghosts and alien visits such a stretch?

And what about the Mayan prophecies of December 2012? Why did the Mayan calendar end so abruptly much like the Mayans themselves? If I were a deity, I would be mighty frustrated by the nightly news and the insidious negativity going on and I might be tempted to say, "That is it. I am done trying to get these people on the right track and to hell with Christmas!"

Alas, sorry to all the doomsday preppers, we are still here. You are still prepared, and the rest of us that at least took note of the warnings, are still committing a slow suicide globally and the homicide of Mother Earth, daily. It has to come to an end someday anyway.

I dunno, she's got gaps, I got gaps, together we fill gaps.
Rocky Balboa character
from the movie *Rocky* (1976)

MARRIAGE

I have been married 4 times. It may be dubious expertise, but I may finally have it right. If any of my exes are reading this— not to worry. It takes two to screw it up. I have had a lot of counseling and "program" (the AA and NA variety), and tons of practice with the resentment prayer.

The last man I married is quiet and not the spontaneous type, an analytical mind, usually a slow burner, but I don't advise you to piss him off. I am garrulous, and sometimes think before I act, but not as often as I should, and I like people not computers (my husband is a computer systems administrator).

Oh, it gets better. He is a registered alien (British) and 18 years younger than I am. It works and I have no packaged answer. Here is what I think might have happened.

1. He loves and respects who I am and vice-versa
2. We are *both* in recovery.
3. I am his polar opposite. (It has been said before that means I am a woman and he is a man). We *would* survive without the other.
4. We disagree, but we talk.
5. I am not crazy about fighting and neither is he.
6. I keep the trying to change him to a minimum, and he doesn't try at all.

Age has nothing to do with it even if I could have given birth to him. Occasionally, when he is listening to AC/DC and I am listening to Motown that seems a bit off, but he is, as they say, "an old soul" and, well, I am old.

Barbara Kemm-Highton

If I were a young adult today, I would think that all families are blended and that marriage is what falls into place directly after an expensive excursion into bridezilla. Besides, the divorce option is always on the table. In my day, and in my home, you married for life, even when you were strangling. Neither one was a great option. I would be ill-prepared for marriage today in my twenties, and I was then.

I squashed my single-world-traveler dreams, which poverty and a heavy dose of partying would have ultimately done anyway and decided I would do what all the 22-year-old brides in the newspaper were doing. I found someone to marry in college who was decent and hard-working. Beyond that I believed that it was my fate or destiny, depending how you look at it, to become a wife and then a mother.

I was told in college that I had better be an English teacher because I wasn't a very good writer. Good thing I was drinking a lot then because being a young high school teacher would prove to be frightening from all angles. I was pregnant the first year of teaching and managed to dodge one bullet— now I had to figure out how to be a parent.

No offense to you, Mom and Dad, you did the best you could given the tools you had, and no blame is cast, but due to your loveless marriage, the depression, the PTSD, the alcohol, and the continuously negative environment that I was raised in, I had very few parenting skills and even fewer insights into the "institution of marriage." (We won't go into the ironies of this particular term).

So, a few years into being a spouse, I kept circling around this relationship—this time with two young children in tow. It wasn't working. There was no connection. I was miserably unhappy and felt pretty guilty about that. Have I mentioned that I was once a Catholic?

Like I said I will not point fingers, but at this time I ran into a man who paid attention to me. Unfortunately, the list of women he paid attention to was longer than his... arm. Serial cheaters stop short of being serial killers, but they still

A Life Winding Down

do a lot of damage, and they are either addicts or sociopaths or both.

I will split hairs here and say that I emotionally cheated and backed off of the ultimate betrayal, but emotional cheating carries some of the same guilt.

All things happen for some bizarre reason, and this time I was to be identified as the latest person he was dallying with, but I wasn't the chief dally. Anyway, all hell broke loose. I can see me raising my hand (student-like) in my mind's eye in a swirl of angry people and meekly protesting. I was still very ashamed of my own behavior and could have stopped that train before it left the station.

So, I needed to air that.

A little more on cheating in general. Killing someone once doesn't make you a serial killer, just as cheating once.....anyway, it is a poor way to end a relationship. It hurts everyone.

Pay attention here and you can learn if you are cheating or thinking of it. It is *self-* destructive, and it is a particular kind of emotional pain that can ruin any chance of parental camaraderie for the children. God forbid you *tell* your children, especially if they had no knowledge anyway, in an attempt to vilify the wandering spouse. You are no better than the cheater in my book and worse—you are venomous.

Now, that said, people make terrible mistakes. If you cannot learn to forgive yourself and others, then you might do what I did. I wasn't high up there on the self-esteem ladder, so I thought I would pick partners later that would contribute to my self-loathing. Sorry guys, alcohol and drug abuse does not make a person a good companion, husband or stepfather. Some of these unions can be really scary. My alcoholism had escalated, and craziness ensued. Let's just say at one point, I could have been seriously harmed.

I stumbled into the program of AA when I was at my emotional and physical bottom. Crawling out of that hole was arduous; the layers were muddy-thick and I felt mired in

Barbara Kemm-Highton

them for a few years. I was vaguely annoyed that these recovering people spoke in bumper stickers, and the program itself had a cult-like air, but ultimately it taught me 12 steps to a sane life. If I had to endure all the sorrow and addiction in my life to come to this kind of clarity, then I am grateful. Regrets? Of, course. My children were present for all of this. I love them deeply and wanted so much more for them than my paralyzed existence.

In the end, practicing the steps, not drinking, praying (to something) and showing up for meetings gave me much more than sobriety. I rediscovered the spiritual being I had always been.

This is where my current husband entered my life. He had already been years on this same journey. It is an old but viable adage that until we are a whole person we aren't ready to have a relationship with another person and, at least in my case, that seems to be true.

The world is a kind of spiritual kindergarten where millions of bewildered infants are trying to spell "God" with the wrong blocks.

Edwin Arlington Robinson

SPIRITUALITY

I will be incensing all the religions in the "Bible Belt," but I have never believed that religion was God-made. Somewhere in catechism class in about middle school, I thought to myself, "I will never make it to heaven even with the confession option." God is so demanding and *angry*, according to the Bible passages being hurled at our young minds, that I might just as well walk out the door in my little blue uniform and commit all manner of sins. I was going to end up in hell anyway or limbo (which seemed worse to me because it was nowhere). I also realized there were some beautiful, lyrical and compassionate passages, too, but since fear keeps the flock in the barn, so to speak, then the seething scripture would be the most effective.

To this day, I have little trust for an ancient text and its questionable translations, not to mention, its varied uses based upon greed, corruption, discrimination and control, but, hey, I could be wrong. Next question for me would be if this is God's word how come other religions have their own bible. A question I had pondered at about 10 and still do. No one has answered it for me either.

Conversations with God by Neale Donald Walsh made a lot more sense to me, but then who is this man who purports to be a portal to God? I also like reading Buddhist texts and the Tao's lyrical poetry, but I must admit that I am not well versed in the Good Book.

Barbara Kemm-Highton

Give me anything that teaches peace, love of others, the universe, the earth, its animals and plants and our connectedness to this Source of pure light and love. Then throw in the power of the mind for healing, and I think I have found *my* God and his/her/its message

As a "good little Catholic" girl, though, I prayed the prayers (in Latin, no less), sang the songs, gave up the meat on Fridays, stayed away from my father's church, and took communion, but let's just say at a very impressionable age, I thought all of it was bunk. Where was the God of love and kindness and compassion and in whose likeness I was made? (In all fairness *he* or *she* probably wasn't worried about hair or weight gain). But then I often pictured my God as a strong black woman reminiscent of my first babysitter who looked, suspiciously, like Aunt Jemima. Her name was Arcola.

Today, globally, we are staging "holy wars." Again! You would think we would have learned something about that oxymoron from our dark and evil history of torture and murder in the name of whose beliefs would dominate the masses. Not so much. The very fact that some of my own hometown religions are openly condemning Muslims and a few fringe fanatics are burning their mosques screams "evil" to me. Who would worship a higher power who upholds discrimination? Apparently, that would be some followers of a powerful local church and a few of their wealthy and equally influential members, a few other entrenched religions, along with some not so mainstream religions (who then scoff at all the other religions). Are we seeing a pattern here?

All of this being said, I do believe there are kind people within these churches who are sure that they have a God who is all loving, and who is the "go to" for life's troubles. Some of these fine people are making blankets for babies, meals for the hungry and homeless, and spreading all manner of kindness in the community. Mother or Father or It, God Bless them.

A Life Winding Down

Where I have a problem is churches that encourage some young person to go to the Middle East or Africa and try to bang a bible over the head of the member of an eastern religion or tribal medicine man and tell them they must convert to Christianity. They are lucky, due to world-wide fanaticism that they aren't beheaded and perhaps some of them are. Didn't all this forced conversion happen to the Quakers and the Native Americans, too? To murder someone for not believing in your religion is the highest form of evil, (but surely these same people were not saying that these vile acts (against the laws of the much-revered commandments) was demanded by their God? Hmm.

Does no one believe in the right to worship (unless it is harming others) is our right as a human being? We are perfectly within our rights *not* to believe in a divine being. It is also our right *not to know* what to believe in. However, congregations that engage in such depraved activities as incest, rape, abuse, mind control, mass suicides, allowing children to die when they need medical help are in no way affiliated with a God. Period! End of discussion.

I also have a problem with churches who give generously to community projects if the hidden agenda is to gather more church patrons by converting the persons they have helped. The end does not justify the means, or it helps them choose a better life. See. I can't make up my mind on this one.

If I am asked what church I go to, and it happens more than I like, I have been unfortunate enough to say "I don't belong to a church." After which someone always declares that I need to go to their church and that I haven't been "saved."

Please! Sticking my head under water will not save me. Random acts of kindness from any human being will go a long way toward saving a person. It is right up there with loving yourself and others.

Barbara Kemm-Highton

These same church-going people believe that a God does not approve of gay people, divorced people, eastern religions, atheists, or agnostics and women who have abortions. Really?

So what do I believe or adhere to or pray to?

First, I cannot meditate well. I have taken classes, set aside time, taken deep breaths until my chest hurt, and I cannot get this right. Then I discovered it is not about right, it is about practice and intention. Most mornings I read *How to Be Compassionate* by the Dalai Lama, *Heart Thoughts* by Louise Hay, *The Great Awakening: Concepts and Techniques For Successful Spiritual Practice* by Dr. Michael Sharp, and *Miracles* by Stuart Wilde (a small book about tapping in to your highest self). I am guessing that your highest self or soul self does not sit in judgment of *anyone*. (Still working on this one though).

I believe in healing yourself with a prism of colors or a white or golden light. I do this when I am stressed or ill. Do I believe in judgment after we die? Yes and No. I am sorry, but what if our creator is all love and forgiveness, in other words, *unconditional love*. What if he or she or they did not create a heavenly penal system more horrendous than anything man could come up with?

What if we are on a karmic wheel until we get it right? What if we are players on a stage acting out hundreds of scenarios and always exercising our free will to make the right choices to evolve our spiritual selves? What if we are genetically engineered players created for the amusement of a far more advanced civilization on another planet?

These are all possibilities to the *open* mind, but beyond our perplexing origins, what about those among us who have committed evil deeds on this earth and have not had to pay, so far. What if Hitler had to incarnate into a promoter of humanity and world peace in a future lifetime? Will he have paid his dues? What if a serial killer incarnates and is then himself murdered in another lifetime? I am just saying.

A Life Winding Down

I choose to believe I am a perfect spirit having an imperfect human experience. I have no clue where the "great beyond" lies. When I die and have my life review, as so many Near Death Experiencers have reported, I hope that I am not cringing at my mindless selfishness here on this earth plane. Or if I am face to face with the planetary council who decided to seed this planet, I might get to ask indignantly "How could you just let us be so stupid?"

Like I said, if you are reading this and I have already "kicked the bucket" (where did this unsavory one come from?), perhaps you can channel me and I will be saying to you "Ah ha! I was right about all of it." Or perhaps I was met by this punishing God who said I was an ogre, and I needed to go to hell and push a rock up a hill over and over again for all of eternity. I think my mythology and early Catholicism are mixing together here. In which case, I am highly preoccupied, but I am hoping for the "Ah ha!" one.

I am not Eckhart Tolle or Iyanla Vanzant or the Dalai Lama or Deepak Chopra or Oprah or even Dr. Oz. I do not hold the keys to the wisdom of life and spirit, but I have learned from all of them. The sum total of what they are saying is that I believe I need to rise above the pettiness of inhabiting this physical body, while still honoring and caring for its maintenance, and go deeper into the source of my being. I do see, with more clarity each day that I am living in an illusion created by like-minds. A simple example would be the constant streaming of thought patterns that occurs daily in all forms of media with the clear message that we are embroiled in endless negative turmoil and worse. We have forgotten to respect ourselves and others, the animals, and the entire living, breathing planet. Some of us have limited experience with the beauty of a quiet time in a forest (hunters do not count since they are stalking and killing) or have walked in a garden where life is at its simplest and most majestic and is doing its rhythmic, earthly job. In those moments when I see natural life with the birds singing and

Barbara Kemm-Highton

trees moving in the wind and I feel the sun warming my face, I know that this is what we really are, and I am a little closer to a heaven.

We never become really and genuinely our entire and honest selves until we are dead -- and not then until we have been dead years and years. People ought to start dead and then they would be honest so much earlier.
                                                                    Mark Twain

DEATH

There is no one to interview about the experience of death, right? That would be wrong. Granted we can ask the proliferation of spiritual or religious leaders, but let's just say if they haven't actually died and returned to tell their tales then they would also fall short. We can ask psychics because they actually talk to the dead. Do you know the origin of the word *psychic?* Its etymology is a Greek word *psychikos* and it means "of the soul." It does not mean charlatan or whack-job. That is not to say that fraudulence and mental illnesses might inhabit the mind and body of some of those claiming to be spirit channels, but usually someone who possesses psychic abilities stands ready to be tested and has some proof. Why else would you put yourself out there to be ridiculed?

The other group of interviewees would be Near Death Experiencers (NDEers). These are estimated to be 15 million strong in the U.S. alone according to an old 1992 Gallup Poll and this 4-18% of the population, roughly 1 in 20 people, appears to be just the ones who are brave enough to share their accounts.

Thanks to authors Dr. Raymond Moody, P.M.H. Atwater, Dannion Brinkley, Melvin Morse, MD, Dr. John Lerma, Dr. Jeffery Long, Dr. Eben Alexander and a host of everyday normal people and small children who have had their stories published, we have a treasure trove of information. If you don't like to read books then go to the internet and look at the stories on the site devoted to the NDE community, *nderf.org*. There are 40,000 and counting to choose from.

The commonality of these shared events is not the standard tunnel and white light symbology, but a united recounting of being met by filmy beings, dead relatives, friends or pets. A sense of peace permeates this other space they occupy as spirit and many do see their spirit guides, angels, Jesus, ascended masters, or a light being that they presume to be God. Most are asked a question about returning to their bodies or are told, "It is not your time." To a person, they all want to stay enveloped in this powerful light that they struggle to define but agree that it is bliss or extreme love. They are able to see everything in an instant and even though many are privy to a review of their lives, they feel that they are observing how they lived, both the good and the bad, without being punished or judged. However, many are able to feel how they may have harmed a person, an animal or Mother Earth herself. Not bad. I could live with this or technically die with this.

But hold on. There are a few these experiencers who have glimpsed a hellish, hideous, and dark underworld. Many of these visions are so frightening that they do have a life changing event, but mainly from the terror of what they witnessed. I am personally holding out that the majority of the NDEs are positive, and we can look forward to shedding this worn old bag of flesh and bones to fly through the universe as our lighter and more enlightened spirit selves.

This information is far better than fearing the inevitable.

I had a pervasive fear of death for many years and would wake up in a cold sweat from frequent nightmares. My father died young and his exit from this life was pretty dismal. He had abused his body for 40 plus years and his lungs became compromised. Watching someone waste away oxygenated, often panicky from the loss of air, has a profound effect on

A Life Winding Down

those trying to care for them. I became very cynical about what is out there to ease us into the transition. I saw the fear in my father's eyes because he wasn't ready to leave and had no control over his impending demise. My father was a veteran of war and probably suffered from PTSD and then surviving those horrors comes the irony of dying from a relentless and undignified illness. I never heard him speak of angels or relatives in his hospital room, but then he slipped into a coma and became brain dead before his organs finally ceased.

My mother succumbed to leukemia. Also, not a pretty disease. She was living her dream close to the ocean, happily married and with lots of friends in sunny Florida. She didn't want to leave yet either. I had an opportunity to talk to her about death, and she asked what I believed. She had been a devout Catholic her whole life, and, at the end, she questioned what she had believed. Since I had a confusing array of beliefs that I didn't want to spring on her at this time, and since I was still researching this to the best of my ability, I was careful not to question a lot of the process she was going through. She opted to be cremated and wanted to know what I thought.

I was uncomfortable at this point and said I thought God was okay with this. She would only have a few weeks left. I came back home after one week since the amazing organization known as Hospice said it could be a month that she could linger, and she died the week after I returned. Lots of regret, followed.

I had the incident in the kitchen the day she died. I was feeling guilty that I had left her. I have her ashes in an ornate box on my desk, but I admit I am unsure where she resides now. My mother and I had a very contentious and dramatic relationship in her lifetime, and unlike many who say they feel their mother and father still around them, I am not so sure. I continue to talk to both of my parents and many other relatives and pets that I can no longer see in this dimension. I have come to believe they do exist in some form somewhere in a parallel or higher vibratory universe. They do occasionally come to me in my dreams, and perhaps this is the portal to keep communication going?

In the midst of voracious reading about the close encounters of others, I lost that fear, but do I know what happens when we die? Do I believe that our culture has it right? I lean much further away from the grim reaper and more toward the ascended beings or family, friends and pets escorting us, but does all of this help when you lose a young child— particularly to a violent death?

All I can share is what I found in some of my research.

1. Some hospice nurses and doctors have claimed to have seen angels or spirits in the room with their dying patient or sensed that another presence was there.
2. Some of the family and caregivers have seen a wisp of white smoke or electric energy arise from the patient's body at the moment of their last breath.
3. A large number of loved ones left behind have been "visited" by their relatives, friends or pets that have passed. There are classic stories by children who have seen grandma or grandpa sitting in their room smiling and saying goodbye and vowing to watch over them, telepathically. Many times these same children were spared the knowledge of the death of their beloved grandparent until they shared this spirit visit.
4. Some of the parents I interviewed for a book about murdered loved ones admitted to visits by their sons or daughters. They were afraid to be seen as crazy, so they did not openly share their experience. Some of them have kept their murdered or missing children's rooms intact and locked and will find objects moved around on a regular basis.

A Life Winding Down

5. NDE participants come back with a purpose to change the world and immerse themselves in charitable acts and do not fear leaving their bodies when they are "called" again. Experiencers often say they are so different they would swear another person is inhabiting their body now.
6. A small number of doctors or nurses or family members have seen a room transform before their eyes, and the spirit of the deceased leave through an opening in the ceiling.
7. NDEers have mentioned that they left their bodies and traveled around hospital wards listening to conversations, and then when they were revived were able to tell the nurses, doctors, patients or loved ones what they had observed. The family and hospital staff were astounded, and a few of them were close to fainting when they heard their private conversations repeated. NDEers also report that they were able to arrive anywhere in a matter of seconds, flying to towns or houses or even to the stars by just thinking about where they wanted to go.
8. We do not appear to shed our bodies and leave this world unassisted.

There are so many stories like this that I am always amazed at the fear and ignorance that is still being taught and reinforced by many who should know better.

I am especially miffed by these idiots (sorry, but you are) who dismiss all manner of death as "God's will." How does this help a parent whose little child was tortured and murdered? I say stop making a god a master tormentor and, well, serial killer.

Is it just possible that there are evil, deranged humans, and we accidentally cross paths with them, or is there more to this? As spirits, could we have chosen a body and knew when we would be exiting? I am not suggesting that we chose a heinous murder, but perhaps we chose a quick exit

Barbara Kemm-Highton

since we were already a highly evolved spirit. I am just saying.

For my family. When I am "at death's door," stay with me. Talk to me, and if I can talk to you please try to listen. I will tell you what I am experiencing. Don't put me in a coma with drugs. Don't tell me to go if I am not ready. Pray that I will still be around you in spirit. Look for me in the flowers, the sun, the butterflies, and all the animals. I will be there. Talk to me after I am gone. I can hear you. Love lives on. Take me home to die.

I will shed this cumbersome bag of wrinkles, thinning hair, and brittle bones. My eternally 30-year-old spirit self will be there to help you cross over when your time comes.

Politics, noun. A strife of interests masquerading as a contest of principles. The conduct of public affairs for private advantage.

Ambrose Bierce,
The Devil's Dictionary

POLITICS

I am so deficient here that I almost didn't include the topic. I am not a political analyst or a sharp-tongued journalist. Partisan politics, at least on the surface for a voter, seems to be crippling a nation.

I am neither a flag waver nor a cross carrier nor a bible enthusiast, all of which seems to penetrate the campaign trail, being followed closely by, of all things, the root of all evil, *money*, (enough to diminish hunger globally), and scathingly negative political ads. Does anyone see the disparate marriage of these two images?

Since the current campaigning in 2016 had reached such an undignified, childish and violent level, I need to urge every human being to consider the fear mongering, racism and gender discrimination going on. The monsters we have created out of fear are well documented in history and we all know the consequences. I propose that if we elect out of fear and misinformation then that is precisely how the dictators will win.

Let's for just a second envision a global interest in saving ourselves from destruction, and I realize how naïve this sounds, but shouldn't any world leader be in office to do the following things?
1. Unearth all corruption.
2. Defend the rights of everyone, including animals.
3. Work tirelessly for peace
4. Work tirelessly to save the physical planet.

Barbara Kemm-Highton

5. Work to end the violence associated with drug trafficking (I am leaning now toward the legalization of *all* drugs).
6. Equalize money so that no one is homeless, hungry, or without medical care.
7. Remove the need for violence in society by spending money on rehabilitation and self-sufficiency instead of worthless campaign ads and funding for politicians.
8. End *all* human trafficking.

I can hear all the clamoring from all the smug intellects and politicians as I am writing this. But listen up. If we created this mess by like-thinking, we can un-create it. We have perpetrated a message of "It will never change," or "This is the way it has to be." We have made it so by affirmations. This is really a simple tool of counseling and motivating a person. Norman Vincent Peale, motivational author, knew it. The book *The Secret* supposedly garnered from an ancient text knew it. The man called Jesus knew it. What is *it?*

Our constant thoughts are powerful. They give us whatever we believe is reality. That would be both *good* and *bad.*

If this is too simple for you, I urge you to write down what kind of society you would like to live in. Unless you are a sociopath and it is all about you, the list will likely be some variation of the list that I wrote. Then beside each one write what you honestly think about each of these Utopian wants coming to fruition. It probably doesn't match.

Do you seriously think that this God that politicians are always making sure we know they believe in, would ignore a request from all of us to change the way we do business thus creating an intelligent, productive, peaceful and equal society? So why are we praying to a light being who says "No" to peace?

A Life Winding Down

My guess is that our thinking "business as usual" has kept us imprisoned for millions of years. It is doing this globally, as well.

Think about this, prayer circles seem to work. Why not a world circle? If we all collectively asked for peace on the planet (do they do this at peace summits?) would that simple prayer be answered? It is certainly worth a try. I actually can hear you mumbling *but*...there are people who feed off of chaos, poverty, drugs, hatred and violence. You might be surprised how much more powerful we would be and their numbers would be small. Besides, if we think our God would buckle to them, then we can't be in the circle anyway.

If this is too much Zen or Dalai Lama for you then consider this. We are a warring society based on a system of gambling, greed, and corruption and where has this taken us so far? Our children are killed in foreign countries, our economy is run by the speculative gambling of the stock market, and drugs, gun violence and poverty are taking down our children and our neighborhoods. I certainly would have the time to ring a few bells and sit down with masses of people for a common goal of love and peace.

To a person this is what all of us, even the worst of us, want. With love, peace will follow. Love is the master healer. Here is an image that I will see in my head forever: A band of American soldiers boarding an Iranian fishing vessel and all the men embracing each other because the Americans, their enemies, had just saved them from an attack by pirates. Now, I am not leaving out the pirates. Given love and a decent living perhaps they would not be doing *this* for a living. All love heals and comes full circle.

I also know what you are saying now. Some people cannot be healed with love and you will use examples of terrorists, drug lords and serial killers etc. Since that has not been tried, how do we know? Am I suggesting that you enter a terrorist compound and say "I love you?" I think that might be considered a suicide mission, but we certainly can pray

Barbara Kemm-Highton

for their souls and send love to them, one person at a time. Wouldn't that work instead of fueling them with hatred. That *has* worked. They hate Americans and other groups of people and we call them "evil" and so on and so on. The rhetoric is endless, the thoughts pervasive, and behold—they are evil and they hate us. So, Politics, like everything else has been created by our thoughts. What a world this could be if we thought "Our policies should be about love and peace."

Too easy? A slogan in AA often used is the definition of insanity "Doing the same things over and over expecting different results."

A person is always startled when he hears himself called old for the first time.
                              Oliver Wendell Holmes

AGING

It is inevitable, but I don't have to agree with it or like it. No, I do not choose the alternative, but what I like the least about it is that my mind seems to be stuck in the 40s, not the 1940s, but *my* 40s. I still think I can water ski and roller skate and dance up a storm; all the while, forgetting that this energetic, muscular mind is perched atop thinning bones, sagging biceps, and wobbly ankles. All of this body and mind disconnection makes for some precarious goals, and visits to the chiropractor.

I will give you the dislikes first and leave the likes for the end. Males will have a different list, but I think all the women are with me here.

1. *Makeup tricks* takes on a whole new meaning. What used to be likened to painting on a canvass becomes finger gymnastics to make sure lines are straight, blush hasn't fallen into a crack and that you resemble an enhanced face, not a circus clown. After all is said and done, you hope you have brightened your color, that you wore your glasses, or used the magnifier, and everything is where it should be. (Remember the skit Carol Burnett used to do on the aging movie star, cigarette in the holder, lipstick askew and false eyelashes sliding away? "Ready for your close-up?" Most ladies of my age have "had work done." Money is a deterrent as is botulism and botched surgery. As of this writing, I have succumbed to some of them. I judge no one who can afford this avenue, by the way, but have since accepted my age and have found a

Barbara Kemm-Highton

reflexology face lift that I do and I have developed a more positive attitude. All of this has helped enormously.
2. Men rarely openly flirt with me. (I can count those times on two hands anyway). They are mostly recently widowed, nearsighted, or younger and almost toothless.
3. Sometimes I ache for no apparent reason. I would like to attribute it to power yoga, but it occurs when I leave the couch to move to the bed.
4. A lot of your friends are using complicated medical terms rather than bargain shopping terms.
5. Dryness becomes associated with more than deodorant.
6. You pass the mirror and think it is someone else who looks vaguely like you.
7. You have to admit you are a senior citizen, or you won't get the discount.
8. You start to regret all the things you haven't done. The proverbial bucket list. (Maybe this is where "kick the bucket" comes from).
9. Memory itself keeps you running a constant game show quiz. You can remember your first grade teacher, but not the person you were just introduced to.
10. Things start to drop—shoulder blades, boobs, chins, cheeks, foreheads, muscles, and they head toward your feet, stopping just short of your orthopedic socks.

Now the short list. Things I like about getting older:
1. I am much calmer and happier.
2. Drama wears me out.
3. I can eat dinner at 4 o'clock in the afternoon.
4. Life becomes a gift, not an endurance round.
5. I appreciate my children and adore my grandchildren.

A Life Winding Down

6. Love between partners has depth and familiarity.
7. Being spiritual becomes a daily elixir.
8. The thirst for knowledge becomes fine-tuned and much more important.
9. Worry becomes a hazard to your health.
10. Simple things like a good book, a good cup of coffee, a warm bed in the winter, my dogs curled up next to me, or a hug from my husband, children, grandchildren or a friend can sustain me for days!

Time to confess. I did have laser surgery when I was 49. My eye bags were falling and I had blue circles underneath them. It might have had something to do with smoking, but like all good addicts, it took me another 3 years to quit. It was the best thing I ever did for myself, others and the environment. A few years ago I tried injections and fillers and it was an expensive vanity that I felt guilty about and stopped. I also tried a tightening laser that I will liken to having your face hit by a stun gun. The jury is still out on this one and it took forever to pay off. I gave up.

Men don't appear to care about lines on their faces. A few in the entertainment business do and we all know how well *that* went. Okay guys, you can get away with wrinkles, but might I suggest man boobs are not attractive. If you have them please stop wearing tight knit shirts or worse, no shirt at all, especially in exotic vacation spots. None of us at a certain age should be exposing our limp or corpulent body parts. Please leave that to the tipsy starlets or ripped 20-year-old gym fanatics.

My favorite joke is: A few old men are sitting around an assisted living facility when they are startled by an elderly naked woman streaking by.

One man says, "What was that?"

Another replies, "I don't know but it sure needs ironing."

It isn't quite as funny in my 70s as it was in my 40s.

*If you bungle **raising** your **children**, I don't think whatever else you do well matters very much.*
                                    Jacqueline Kennedy Onassis

RAISING CHILDREN

There is no playbook and if there were, the rules keep changing. *Now* I think I know how to raise children, and that is the irony of old age. You raise them with care and love and discipline based on basic common sense.

If I ever had any a do-over, it would be this particular life job—raising my children. When I was in an unhappy marriage with a job, school, and a budding addiction to alcohol, (I only stopped when I was pregnant), I had no clue. I knew how to change diapers and to feed and to watch over them to keep them from harm, but do you realize how many people do not even have these rudimentary skills? Infants are placed in car seats in sweltering hot vehicles or left in cars while parents go to convenience stores, or, worse yet, bars, or are left to the care of dangerous babysitters (usually drug addled or sociopathic predators in the guise of a boyfriend). All this being said, I was a hit-and-miss parent when my children needed consistency. It is a disservice to a child to over discipline or under discipline at a whim. It suggests that the parent or parents' needs have not been recognized and is a sure sign of, at best, immaturity, or at worst, a maladjusted being in charge of our smallest and most vulnerable humans, our own kids.

Much has been written about raising a child—spank, don't spank, time out, taking away privileges, and on and on, but much of the rhetoric alludes to the bad behaviors and while I think there are a few teens in this world who deserve a whack, I do not endorse violence at any age. It causes

Barbara Kemm-Highton

violence, fear and often unresolved anger. Are these reactions what you want your child to take into the world? If they are, my friend, then you should not have either children or pets and you need a good therapist.

Here are some of the don'ts first:
1. Don't abuse alcohol and or drugs in front of your children (including cigarettes). They are more likely to emulate what they are taught. If you are saying that this is your right as a parent to abuse chemicals and burn out your lungs, you don't deserve these little people. You are an addict and incapable of giving them the love, protection and care that they need. You can't even do this for yourself!
2. Beatings are abuse and destroy the self-worth of any child. They learn that they are not loved and they are more likely to beat your grandchildren. It makes no difference that this is the way you were raised. At your core you have to know that this is wrong. Abused children *can* grow up to be decent people, but more than likely you are training them for prison—not life.
3. All children want praise and hugs. If you call them… "worthless, fat, stupid, lazy," etc. and you cannot hold them in your arms when they need your comfort, then you may be a sociopath. You are dangerous to your children. Don't have children, but if you do already let someone take over who can teach them self-esteem and love. What you will create is another sociopath to unleash on society. I am well aware that many children can overcome an abusive parent or parents, but why take the chance. Interview any prisoner to find out how they were treated as a child. Damn few had loving, non-violent caregivers.
4. Don't raise your child in a religious cult. They will need a lifetime of therapy for the brainwashing and

A Life Winding Down

the abuse that is inherent in any religion that excuses its behaviors based on a fictitious god who allows loss of any freedoms, sexual abuse, extreme control, fear, isolation, loss of social interactions, severe disciplines, freedom of speech and thought, lack of medical interventions, etc. The sad reality is that most people in cults are unable to see the damage being done to their children because of all these actions listed above. Cult members have to recognize the evils of a mind controlling form of religion. For those who escape, many are trying to help others in the same situations and this is their truly God given life plan. If you are in a cult and can see through it, contact the police or family services. You are a witness. Get your own children out quickly. Seek help. Some of these groups have killed members who try to leave or abuse their children further. There is such a rampant "hands-off " policy toward the right to worship, that we have as a society missed an opportunity to save children from something as sinister as an abusive cult. I was raised Catholic, and I no longer practice and I am not singling out one religion, there are many others, but the abuse of young boys was covered up by the Vatican for years, and I am reasonably sure this is only the very tip of that iceberg. We need to do more to protect all children in religious based situations. The right to parent and worship is not the right to control and abuse, and they are not mutually exclusive.

5. Throwing lots of money at your kids, even if you are able to, is keeping them irresponsible and emotionally crippled. Bailing a child out of every consequence will keep them begging at the door for all of their life or possibly incarcerated. They cannot bypass accountability.

6. If your child, young or old, has a mental illness and is dangerous to you and others, you *must* find help. You cannot engage with a violent personality disorder. This is such a tricky one. In light of the recent school shootings, the most heartbreaking scenario is to love your child, and it is not enough to save him or her from harming others and him or herself. The majority of these lost souls are males and parents need to keep asking for help. I am also aware that many of these parents have been reaching out in frustration to find that assistance and that is too late when it becomes headline news. Their child will then be demonized for the heinous acts committed while they were mentally deficient long before this occurred. We need to find better resources and monetary help for these families and their potentially scary children. If you are a parent in this situation lobby, lobby, lobby. Get this out in the media. Network and post information. There is power in fighting and power in education.
7. Teach your daughters and sons about "stranger dangers" even in their teens and older and how to protect themselves. An eighteen-year-old girl out at night by herself jogging or walking from a party alone to a car, or worse yet drinking under age and in the dark alone is pretty much insane. It is also becoming unsafe for boys and young men. The dangers do not just lurk at night. With many predators out hunting, be aware of your surroundings in the light of day.

   I am not a fan of arming yourself, but mace, stun guns and self-defense classes can be better than nothing. All children and teens should know what to do if they are kidnapped or an assault is attempted.
8. Poverty can breed abuse and neglect, but lack of money cannot be used as an excuse. Some of my friends who were raised in homes where money was

A Life Winding Down

scarce, but love was abundant are some of the best people in the world. That is not to say you can't be wealthy and loving, but the simpler and more appreciative the environment, sometimes the closeness of a meal or a movie or card game or sharing stories around a family event becomes the cornerstone of the strength in that person. It builds safety and character to know that kind of closeness.

9. Don't teach your children to be sexually active by being promiscuous yourself. Males and females. Your kids will know. It becomes very generational to have babies when you are too young. Once again most teen mothers do not want their teens to be mothers or fathers, but they need to show them that it is not the norm.

    Okay, Moms out there, if you have 6 children by 6 different fathers and you cannot afford to raise them, I am not judging you, but try to break that cycle now and do not have a number 7. You may love your kids, but you are overwhelmed and that will have a profound effect on who they are and who they become. Enough said! In the land of sexual protection every tree has a condom or anti-pregnancy device, morning after help etc. No excuses. Once you do have them, follow all of the dos and don'ts listed to the best of your ability. Let any father that is a good guy help you out.

10. Think before you have a child with someone who is abusive to you. If it is too late, seek help for the child having contact with this person, especially a daughter.

The list of dos has been around for eons:
1. Love and protect your children.
2. Show them how to work and love and give back to the world.

3. Accept that they will make mistakes. Forgive them and have fair consequences for their actions.
4. Love them unconditionally, but this does not mean to indulge all of their wants.
5. Teach them to value all others including animals (the abuse of animals is a huge red flag and can indicate a budding dangerous personality), the world itself, and its gifts and themselves.
6. Ask for help if you cannot raise your child properly, or you are afraid that he or she has serious problems. *Any* child is a gift.

Now and then it's good to pause in our pursuit of happiness and just be happy.

Guillaume Apollinaire

HAPPINESS

I wanted to be pretty and skinny and that would make me happy. I said this to my overweight self in the mirror when I was 16 years old. I looked around at some of my friends and they were tall, slender, and athletic and could wear all the newest styles without looking chubby or dumpy. My nickname in high school became Bubbles for my burgeoning girth and false "bubbly" personality. I had been both of these, slender and attractive, a combination of my mother and father's good looks and physiques, when I was younger and through junior high school. In high school, I had a series of mysterious physical changes. I began to gain weight even though I was not an overeater. I developed blemishes and my hair became coarse and brittle, not to mention, profuse sweating became a daily companion. I stopped having periods and was often highly constipated. My depression was obvious, and I turned that anger mostly inward but outward in the tense living conditions of my parents' unhappy marriage. (As an adult, I would stumble across an article about thyroid disease, which later became my diagnosis, and its relationship to the practice of treating sinusitis with Radium Iodine tubes placed in the nose. I was treated with this method in 1960 at 14 thus killing my healthy thyroid. (The practice was banned in 1962).

Having an answer and a solution for my bewildering conditions *might* have made me happy, but from this vantage point, I realize, once we have what we think will make us happy, we move on to the next thing.

Barbara Kemm-Highton

Toward the end of four years of an exhausting run on speed dating, mountains of beer bottles, research paper deadlines, holding down a job, and finals week, better known as college, I thought marriage would make me happy. So I did that.

I had a teaching job, but as any green high school teacher knows, *that* won't make you happy. I had my moments in my 34 years of teaching that I loved what I did, but teaching did not make me happy either, and at the end of my career, I loved the kids, but I was weary, not happy.

So, my own kids would make me happy. I had been an only child. This had to do it for me. Unhappy marriage and kids is not an equation for happy. I was caught up in a cycle of being stuck in a loveless marriage (isn't this what my parents also had?) and not loving myself and trying to love my kids. So, I was skinny again from taking thyroid meds, working full time with junior high kids, taking care of my own kids, medicating myself with alcohol and pills, and trying to stay married. I ended up in the psych ward, but no one there asked me if I was happy; they wanted to know how much I drank so they could send me home with depression meds. Depression meds did *not* make me happy. Perhaps, drinking while taking them had something to do with it.

So, now if I could get out of this marriage, *then* I would be happy. I got out of the marriage, and since teachers' yearly salaries had not even moved up to $16,000 a year, I had a new something to chase to be happy. Money! I was not chasing copious amounts; I just needed enough to survive and raise two kids. I went from seeking happiness, to just making it through the week.

I escaped into alcohol and had a botched tubal surgery that nearly took my life. Happy was a word for other people's lives. Hell, I was lucky just to get up in the morning and get home to a can or five of beers a night.

I am guessing that my kids were not happy either. I was struggling financially. They did not see enough of their

A Life Winding Down

father, who resented me and had remarried, and I had had an extended hospital stay because of a malpractice worthy surgery. An NDE might have helped, but even though a priest was called in after a second surgery for the peritonitis that had ravaged my body, I only recall a pervasive darkness while I was under.

I had a temporary colostomy and a recovery time of several months and a third surgery. If I was chasing money, I was going backward. My salary was reduced and I now owed exorbitant medical bills. I sued because it was my only option for the bills.

Are we happy now? I lost the lawsuit and my second marriage too was failing. I was on the road to bankruptcy and I was still a practicing alcoholic. My children were sad and unhappy and reacting to the choices of the adults in their lives. This was not a ride on the happiness bus.

Even I began to see this pattern of living as ludicrous and self-destructive. Sadly, things did not improve for a few more years. I was not ever happy because I always thought what was outside of me would make me happy. The key to all of this was to *make me* happy. You can't force unhappy to be happy.

It was me who was unhappy living in my own skin, consumed with guilt and alcohol and the prevailing thought that something was wrong with me internally. I had no idea that I could simply ask for help from whatever was out there.

Today, I have grown to be happy. I choose to be happy a good part of the time, and I attract many good things to myself. Not being addicted went a long way toward discovering my soul. It is the soul that we seek for our happiness.

Externals, like having wonderful sons (in spite of what I did to screw them up) and amazing granddaughters, a husband I respect and love, a home, some money, pets, and retirement are wonderful, but they are not the core of my happiness. I now believe that I am a child of the universe and

Barbara Kemm-Highton

happiness is my right in life. I expect struggles, but I *deserve* happiness. My job is to share it with the universe: with every person, animal and plant that I encounter.

The art of medicine consists of amusing the patient while nature cures the disease.

                                                            Voltaire

HEALTH

Veteran newsman Walter Cronkite once said, "America's health care system is neither healthy, caring, nor a system." The debate rages on and on, fodder for politics, often exposed as corrupt, for profit, and run mainly by powerful pharmaceutical and insurance companies. Dying in other words is big business. Look at your hospital bills. Pay attention to many highly marketed drugs that had to be pulled because they were killing people, but not until they killed *enough* people. Observe the fact that alternative medicine, naturopaths, chiropractors and acupuncturists are minimally covered by insurance, if at all. Take a close look at all the people who flood emergency rooms because they have nowhere to go for heart attacks, strokes and accidents. Take a look at the OTC industry and the many side effects of these *legal* drugs as well. The overuse of acetaminophen, which we were all told to give our babies, can kill a person if it is overused. The rampant use of antibiotics is now a major health issue.

    I do not mean that traditional medicine should be totally scrapped, but let's move back to the real culprit here. It is the food industry as much as it is the over prescription of drugs. In order to fill our shelves with non-perishable goods, they began to stuff foods with sodium, chemicals and useless fats so that in the event of nuclear war and the passing of a number of years, many of these items would still be around, albeit past the due date, but able to eat. At what cost to our bodies? It seems to be no accident, and the conspiracy

Barbara Kemm-Highton

theorists have a more ominous reply— perhaps our food supply is dangerous so that we will need doctors and medicines for our many diseases. In other words, our food supplies including produce and animals and all foods with abnormal shelf lives are purposely contaminated for natural selection and for the ongoing profits of health care! Pretty scary, huh? The problem is most of us do not believe it.

Luckily, with the advent of every conceivable television show about healthy diets and weight and the resurgence of home grown foods, farmers markets, and fitness importance, we are taking matters into our own hands and becoming a nation of health reforms. We need to do much more.

That said, the alternative medicine business is expensive and profitable and downright confusing. So where do you go if you are ill?

I still have a general practitioner, but often they want you to take statins or any new drug that helps with high cholesterol and osteoporosis. Many will send us through a battery of tests and tell us that what we have is benign or non-existent or worse yet— a mystery. Thus, the bill for an MRI or the exposure to radiation.

If I go alternative, then it has been suggested that red rice yeast, guggul for cholesterol or calcium and D3, as well as, some very expensive bone supplements will work for the osteoporosis.

Someone suggests yoga or weight bearing exercises (which I already do). Another tells me to eat 6 prunes a day for bone health with stomach wrenching results. Another naturopath says that natural progesterone is best for both symptoms. All of these people are well meaning, I might add, and trying to help. Naturopaths may order expensive tests or x-rays that are not covered by any insurance.

I have had side effects from some of the above natural remedies or cannot take them with thyroid meds (due mainly to my own research), which I have to take since I no longer

A Life Winding Down

have a functioning thyroid. Some of these supplements or tests, I simply cannot afford.

So, anyone who is poor cannot get help in any direction traditional or alternative and what is collected at food banks for them? You guessed it—canned foods lined with BPA and high sodium and other chemicals or foods that will have a longer shelf life than than some of us. Food banks are thankfully being given produce and healthier options but often canned goods are their only choices on their strictly donation budgets. We need to *all* be contributing to feed the hungry.

By the way, have you ever seen such an outrage over a sugar filled, piece of cake that has virtually no benefit to our body (in fact the opposite) being removed from the shelves and touted as a *food* item? They have been brought back by popular demand. Where were these people when cantaloupes and baby spinach were being pulled because of e-coli. We certainly have priority issues, and while I have nothing against mindless sweets, I would not stage something close to a war protest if some of them disappeared.

Here is a novel idea. Make sweets with healthy, but tasty ingredients that are safe to eat. There are some of these out there, by the way, but they are not as heavily supported and marketed. Money is also an issue. They cost more to make and purchase. And who gets left out? You guessed it. We continue to covertly discriminate against the poor by making health unaffordable! In defense of my outrage, there are wonderful people out there who are doing gardens and farmers' markets in inner cities, bringing clean water to impoverished countries, demanding contaminants be removed from foods, etc. but there should be tons of us working to ensure food safety for all.

Meanwhile, drug providers, legal and illegal are becoming wealthy on the backs of *all of us.*

So what exactly do any of us do if we are sick? Dare I say a certain party is railing against the Affordable Health

Barbara Kemm-Highton

Care Act (dubbed Obama Care) and it has its flaws, but at least someone had taken a step to reach the previously uninsured or denied population! We just need to demand not only care for all, but better (non-insurance and pharmaceutical company driven care), as well. We need affordable **disease** control! At this writing premiums are increasing and the population wants to keep their care but for Congress to fix the flaws. Instead the parties are not able to come together and the party in power has been trying to make it fail with no back up plan. Where are "we the people" in this equation?

The term disease when divided into syllables is "dis-ease." Is this a coincidence or a hidden meaning?

I have no answer for a perfectly healthy, vegan, runner who collapses on a 5K run and has a massive heart attack. The term dis-ease does not seem to apply, but then do we use this isolated incident as an excuse to eat fast foods daily and drink liters of soda while watching endless hours of television or sitting at the computer smoking cigarettes?

I have spent a lot of time researching various ailments and find that there are few options other than traditional doctors or health food stores for help. Experimenting on yourself at the advice of a health food store worker can become very costly and possibly dangerous. I still do it occasionally and I do find some herbs or amino acids that help. I also have various tests like mammograms and colonoscopies and thyroid medicine checks with blood tests, and if I would happen to pass out somewhere or have chest pains, you better believe I would let them run those tests—radiation or not! Our options have become so limited.

Anyway, let's see if we can reason through this elusive term "dis-ease." We live on a polluted and unstable planet (that instability caused by humans). We breathe exhaust fumes and factory pollution. We cut down trees and we smoke chemicals. We eat chemicals and live in a high stress

A Life Winding Down

environment based on our jobs and a fractured economy. We take in chemicals that are legal or illegal.

Is there anyone who believes that eating well and exercise is the total answer to a healthy life? Granted this is a huge step, but if the above conditions are ignored, then we are the proverbial fish swimming upstream.

There is a whole school of thought that our bodies were designed to live well beyond 100. In a safe environment with safe foods and no stressors, that could be the norm. Of course, the whole present day health care industry and proliferation of elderly care facilities would be non-existent. I say good riddance. If you tell me these create jobs, I will counter with a lot of anger and abuse being delivered to patients being cared for by minimum wage earners who hate their jobs and their clients. Those same people paid well and trained well could still be elderly caregivers, and they might be more compassionate. The ones who are scary need not apply. The same would apply to doctors and nurses. They would be schooled in all types of medicines that nature has to offer of the non-synthetic variety and be able to direct patients to other therapies including stress relief, non-invasive surgery, acupuncture, reflexology and, and, and…..*the power of the mind to heal.*

No longer would hospitals focus on fountains and marble entry ways and expensively paid CEOs and media reps. For that matter, a comfortable room with aroma therapy and some soothing colors, memory foam bedding and "temporary guests" would help the patient recover quickly enough to go home. Hospitals are expensive, generically decorated hotels designed to be loaded with disposable sheets and a myriad of cleaning chemicals. Who can get well there? And they are the primary place to contract an infection like MERSA or any kind of other invasive infection. I will take bed bugs over this!

Barbara Kemm-Highton

I am fully aware that many people recover and eventually go home, but what do most of them say. "I hate hospitals. I don't want to die there." With good reason.

I visited a fellow teacher in the hospital one time who was bloated with cancer and drugs. She said to me, "They are killing me with chemotherapy." She died the next day, and I *never* forgot her last words.

I know I digress a great deal, but the angels or guides or aliens I listen to for this information (you thought I came up with this by myself? ☺) are talking all at once. I want to address the whole healing with the mind. I believe it is the secret answer and now I have made all health care providers including alternative therapies irate. Sorry, but I suspect that we can think ourselves well. I know you are angry, shaking your fist and pointing out all the sick and dying children at St. Jude's but this is the answer I have been given.

I have also been told that many of us have a shorter time on earth that we actually chose for ourselves, and no amount of positive thinking can change that. So, you ask, why even try to heal yourself? Simply, because you don't know what ending your spirit chose for this body. Move on to healing yourself with your thoughts. If it doesn't work, then you did choose to go wherever we go. If it does, then it does. I think all of it is divinely inspired and freely given to us.

As a child, I developed asthma. I had no insight into why. I had lots of allergies and illnesses and I was told it was hereditary. I also had nightmares and was very fearful and saw dark shadows in my room at night. I was an angry and anxious only child, very thin with deep blue circles under my eyes. Today, I see a connection with depression and anger to my illness. I had no help for my emotional state and that child stayed with me into adulthood. Allergies and sinusitis followed, as well.

In my teen years, a doctor treated my sinus problems with radium iodine. I do not think all doctors are inept, but this practice was later banned because of the damage to a

A Life Winding Down

very important gland we have called our thyroid. My lifelong thyroid issues ended in Graves Dis-ease. Knowing what I know now, I might have opted for another therapy to combat this illness instead of the total removal of the gland. It has been a juggling act to supplement the absence of a gland that can regulate, among other things, your metabolism and your mood.

Side note: I have to fight most doctors to be able to take Armour or Nature-Throid, considered natural thyroid pills. Most of them prefer me to be on a variation of the one size fits all, synthetic thyroid, (a hugely profitable, chemically produced supplement that has made its producer wealthy. According to a Forbes estimate, in the billions). I was forced back on a synthetic drug by a preferred drug list for patients over 65 and a doctor who refused to look at my long history of problems with synthetic thyroid meds, and I was cornered by a market that is run by powerful drug lobbyists and a health care system run by profits and not always patient care.

But here is where I thought things had taken a somewhat mind over matter turn. I had nagging physical problems and suspected my dose of thyroid was off. I was told every time in a blood test that it was in the normal range, but my intuition said otherwise. Then fate stepped in and my hair started falling out (it takes vanity to get us really motivated). I began to ask for that divine kind of help and soon I had a new doctor and a new dose of natural thyroid. I pretty much accepted the answered prayer was my new female doctor. Then I was referred to a specialist. This particular male doctor would not allow me to take the natural thyroid, again!

Fortunately, after writing many letters and making many phone calls of appeal to be involved in my own care, I am full circle. I had to leave the medical system I was in and the Universe or whatever answered my call for help. I had become increasingly symptomatic on the standard medicines and asked for my old thyroid back. I was stone-walled throughout this medical system and then an angel, in a local

Barbara Kemm-Highton

doctor owned hospital, disguised as a nurse practitioner waved a wand and returned me to my meds. Were it only that simple? Our choices are limited here. The pill that I am taking involves using a desiccated pig thyroid. I am so against the wanton destruction of animals that this leaves me heartbroken but was ill enough on all synthetics to surrender. Due to insurance whiplash I have had to return to the original system and I now have an NP that is working with my needs. I am grateful, but we should *all* have so many more choices and more doctors who lend an ear to our symptoms.

I fear that I am not alone in this maze of healing. So you say why didn't I just "think" myself well? If the mind controls *all* illnesses then why are we so reluctant to practice it? Perhaps the only ones who do this successfully even though it is in reverse are hypochondriacs who think themselves ill.

War... Huh... Yeah! What is it good for? Absolutely nothing!
> Written by Norman Whitfield and Barrett Strong and performed by The Temptations and Edwin Starr among others.

WAR

The song was about Vietnam, but the hard-hitting lyrics still reverberate today. It is not my intention to discredit *any* veteran of *any* war, and I am the daughter of a vet, but this has got to stop. My father was an emotional cripple after World War II, not to mention an alcoholic. He killed and watched people die in horrific ways and lost his best friend to The Battle of the Bulge. He feared having a male child to send into war. He remained depressed for most of his life. My mother stated clearly that she married one person and another came back from the war. I lost two friends to the Vietnam War physically and many more mentally.

Veterans remain homeless, jobless, legless, armless and mindless. How can we send our children toward the enemies we have made and have them blown to bits or crippled for the remainder of their lives?

I also know the main line of defense is that we have to be prepared for attack. Be careful all you freedom fighters and flag wavers. Something more sinister may lurk below the surface.

In a very recent interview a current politician was asked about the blatant nuclear threats by North Korea being made by its dictatorial 33-year-old president. In essence he warned us to be careful. "Many wars have been started by accident." That was a frightening admission, but it is very true, and as we now know, many more were started by deception. We

Barbara Kemm-Highton

can continue to debate the whole Iraq war weapons of mass destruction thing, but the fact remains that a country was invaded based on false or faulty intelligence. It is still not doing well as a country and as John Stewart pointed out recently many American still believe that Sadam Hussein had such weapons and that many more believe he was behind the World Trade Center attacks. Propaganda anyone?

If you can stomach the documentary *Why We Fight*, although it is several years old, I highly recommend it. Interviewed are John McCain, Gore Vidal and other experts who contend that the business of war depends on the misleading of the public and the bending of the truth for America's status as a formidable world power, not to mention the weird bedfellows we make to protect our interests in the regions where oil is gold.

So let's relearn. Greed powers the economy and War. How could these go wrong?

I understand the need to protect if others are armed. But would they be armed if we were not threats to one another? If we were all peaceful, then all of the violent methods that we use to "promote peace" would be unnecessary. What would all those generals do? How about all the Oppenheimers? The scientist behind the A-bomb, by the way, was already regretting the monster he had helped to create before it was dropped on all the innocents of Japan.

There are still Americans who are prejudiced against the Japanese for Pearl Harbor! My very uninformed friends, you need to learn your history. You have forgotten Hiroshima and Nagasaki. We have asked these people for forgiveness, by the way. You don't do that if what you did was right.

I have talked to many veteran friends who were brainwashed into becoming a killing machine who committed atrocities in villages akin to My Lai, but it never made the news. Forget that soldiers are represented as tough but gentle, armed but sensible, valiant but vulnerable. There is not a lot of room for developing these antonyms. Many

A Life Winding Down

soldiers do come into villages all over the world with open hearts for the natives who are caught in a conflict they abhor, but when you are *trained, programmed, brainwashed, desensitized* whatever you want to call it, you can harm the very people you are supposedly sent there to protect. There are men and women all over the globe who have gunned down their own comrades or indigent innocents in conflicts that are rife with human errors and rampant fear. They are basically trained to bring down the enemy or be killed and often they can fire at the wrong target. I am sure the Pat Tillman family can attest to the loathsome term "friendly fire." Add to the melee those soldiers who have a psychological break or have *snapped* and begin to randomly attack villages or the actual sociopaths who have signed up. Remember, sociopaths are often charismatic leaders without a noticeable conscience and you have the perfect setting for evil and violence.

Many soldiers can see through the haze of being a freedom fighter and come home to realize that they were *used* to promote a cause that may have had confusing merit and no amount of medals or honors can wipe out the horrors of their dead friends and missing limbs and the seething hatred of their enemies. It was truly a hell on earth.

We have so many veterans that are homeless and without jobs, adequate health care, and adequate psychological care, it isn't any wonder that they have a huge suicide rate. It can, unfortunately, turn to homicide as well. If you are a veteran and proud of what you accomplished and think that I am undermining your service please know that I respect your journey, but it has not been the same for many, many others.

So, what is the answer? Start electing people who are peace brokers not war mongers.

Take a real close look at why we are on this planet earth. If you believe in a divine order of things how can you possibly believe that a god put us here to kill each other?

Barbara Kemm-Highton

Intelligence plus character-that is the goal of true education.

Martin Luther King Jr.

EDUCATION

From wherever he is these days, Doctor King might have some pretty mixed emotions about the way we are educating our youth or anyone for that matter. He saw the pendulum swing toward equality in education, but has it really? Ethnically speaking diversity itself should be an education, but there are those *people* (and I use the term lightly) who still believe that white is superior. Are we all laughing when a White Supremacist comes out on the porch of his trailer with tobacco juice on his shirt standing next to his bedraggled wife and hollow-eyed children looking like extras from the movie *Deliverance* and openly admits, albeit in a toothless television interview that he believes schools should still be segregated?

I know you resent my typecasting here, but let's face it there are a lot of racists still in the world and some are ignorant whites and others are sporting suits and ties. For a myriad of reasons, many poor black and Hispanic children are attending underfunded, poorly staffed, and dangerous schools relegated to their gang and drug infested neighborhoods. How fair is this? And more importantly whose fault is this?

I am going to suggest that many ethnicities blame the inner city culture itself for such neighborhoods and schools, but I applaud the many cities and their educators who are trying to change this dynamic. No one should consider inner city schools someone else's problem. In poverty and drug areas, where children struggle to become somebody, there is anger and a sense of abandonment. Those same children learn to survive every day, but for each child attempting to leave the streets there are 5 more *have-nots* banding together to take their anger out on the *haves*. Throw some serious drugs and weapons into the mix and all of us are in danger. Where do the street criminals go to commit most of their crimes? They come to anyone out there who has anything they have been denied which is a quality education, money, love and the dignity of a good job.

They are pissed off and now devoid of emotion or so jacked up on drugs and trigger happy that anyone in the neighborhood or out of it is in danger. Okay, so you are saying they have a choice and I agree to a point.

Here is the reality. Does the fact that most drugs are moved through inner cities bother you? Yes, there are high rolling drug dealers that are the children of professionals too, but initially and more often the gangs move the drugs through the poverty areas, because money is desperately needed at any cost. When the drugs come, the kids see how to better the poverty temporarily and the culture of prison life is pretty much accepted as well. So, a young poor person in a dismal environment can make a cartel some money. He or she may die in a gun battle with a rival or go to prison, but the money is made and another desperate kid will step up. They are disposable. Does this smack of social cleansing?

Until we are *all* divine children in our own eyes there will be this huge chasm between the poor and those who are able to live comfortably. We create this problem on every level including education with our continued segregationist ideas.

But, the system is broken for all of us as well. I spent 34 years as an educator and came away thinking that this broken wheel needs a tire change. We are letting legislators and administrators dictate a curriculum that fosters disrespect and disillusionment. We care about funding and put our emphasis on statewide testing to achieve the funding. And we are still

A Life Winding Down

low on the totem pole of scores! Here is a litmus test. Try finding out how many kids *like* school (for the education, not the socializing). Most kids do not like school. And when did we as teachers get out of the business of being influential in character building (parents included). There are teachers sleeping with students. There are coaches verbally abusing their players and demeaning them as human beings. There are many teachers who don't like their jobs. Teachers are flaunting their drinking habits and texting their students or worse.

Please, Teachers of the Year or any unsung hero who devotes 10 plus hours a day to kids don't email me. I know you are out there in huge numbers and the crazies are a smaller circle, but dedicated loving people like you are facing overcrowded classes, lack of supplies, demands of standardized testing, and parents who do not support your efforts. Then throw in the discipline that has become a joke, and I am not sure how you roll out of bed every day. I guess all of this is the payback for your salaries rising from poverty level.

Since I am one of you, I will say that, although it is better, education and buildings suitable for that education comes back to money. When kids are not there you lose money, so the cycle of disruptive and perhaps abusive students is in motion. I hear of teachers who are repeatedly kicked by emotionally disturbed students that continue to be reinstated in their classrooms, and, as a mother and a teacher, I cannot see how this benefits anyone. How is being abused everywhere else in the world a crime, but not in the classroom?

I have no answers except to say that children need to be protected from those who are violent and are bullies and teachers need to be protected from them also, parents need to support the good teachers, classrooms should be no more than 25 kids and perhaps any useless spending at any level should be funneled into all schools so that they are not

Barbara Kemm-Highton

hazardous to anyone's health. Many old schools still have crumbling walls, faulty plumbing and heating, dangerous chemicals, and on and on.

Yet, in spite of all the above, kids are still learning.

I am going to make them all (parents and teachers) mad now, but let's only send kids home at night with one good book (or Kindle) to read instead of 3 hours or more of homework every single night. What is the point? If you do your job in class then why is this necessary? I believe that there is too much out there. It is overkill and over stressing most students.

I know that the parents of all the budding doctors and lawyers are aghast and their child is college bound. Here is a thought. College needs to be interactive, less stressful and they also need to quit piling it on, as well. I did not retain the overkill from a higher education and would have appreciated less homework since I also had to work to pay for books and tuition. If this does not apply to you then I commend you, but stress did not build my character or enhance my store of knowledge. Likely our students everywhere would like to learn, build character, and have some marketable job skills. One size does not fit all, but that is how we tend to teach and test.

There are tons of monies out there flowing into the machinery of war, oil companies, pharmaceutical giants, and political ads while many schools are crowded, structurally and environmentally unsafe, and in some cases run by dangerous students. And of this writing the March for Life is taking place since more students have been gunned down by an emotionally unstable student with access to an assault rifle entering their environment and snuffing out their lives. This is ludicrous. Our love of being armed and ignoring mental illness is killing our students.

The system remains out of balance because we believe we cannot change the system. The safety of a student is necessary for them to learn as is the acceptance of equal

A Life Winding Down

education for all. Education is yet another by-product of what we have accepted as a democracy and continue to believe that the people who run our state and federal governments are doing all that they can. That belief has crippled us. Put the flag down. Love America, but resolve to make the system change for our kids, for their education, and for their future. Tell your Congressperson that you want money to better your schools and no one should have to send their child to school and have them never return.

When the agenda is profit, greed shows up wearing a grin and a black cape and anyone's child is in danger.

When money flows to fund sports (I am not against sports, but against the hideous salaries of the professionals) at the expense of education then the priorities are always skewed. Until we balance all money for the betterment of society not the lining of someone or some organization's pockets our values will suffer, our education will be second rate, and our most needed professionals will move on.

We have created the education we regard as so important, but not important enough to gift to everyone in a safe environment.

The ego is the false self-born out of fear and defensiveness.

John O'Donohue, *Anam Cara:*
A Book of Celtic Wisdom

EGO

The free online dictionary by Farlex defines ego in three separate ways: *"**1.**The self, especially as distinct from the world and other selves. **2.**In psychoanalysis, the division of the psyche that is conscious, most immediately controls thought and behavior, and is most in touch with external reality. **3.a.** An exaggerated sense of self-importance; conceit. **b.** Appropriate pride in oneself; self-esteem."*

I have no insight into this part of our mental and emotional makeup, so I will freely rely on the experts. I have at times commented on those who have inflated egos from my perspective, but I also know that in our society ego is the touchstone of identification. The physical world reveres beauty and celebrity and all of us become focused on how we look in that tell-all companion to the ego—the mirror!

Unfortunately, even that can lie to us if we have an eating disorder or BDD (Body Dysmorphic Disorder).

If ego is only the third definition (b), then it is a healthy adjunct to our overall acceptance of self. If it is the third definition (a), then the ego has become a narcissistically controlling appendage and has possibly made us dangerous in some situations.

So, do we try to harness or develop our ego?

Even that appears to be a conflict of definitions, so I will defer to the first expert Eckhart Tolle, the author of *A New Earth*. (A book that I read and I am now re-reading). I refer you to this book or the online comments made by the author for Oprah's Life Class. (Eckhart, I will summarize your thoughts so please don't sue me if I miss the mark). Tolle believes that ego is more protective than sinister. We develop a sense of separateness and blaming others to protect our fragile ego selves. The end result is gossiping about others, finding others at fault, (Are we paying attention here all reality shows, especially the housewife and bachelor shows?) and in all situations secretly believing that you are different from the masses because *they* have caused your deep sense of inferiority. Some world leaders may be profiled here. According to Tolle, this is how you know your ego controls you firmly. So if your daily thoughts are: "I am not attractive enough. I never get ahead. Everyone is holding me back from being my better self," then you need to lose such repetitive mantras wrapped in negativity.

So, do you go to war with this thing called ego? The trick seems to be to accept whatever is going on without negative judgment. For example, I wrote a book that I edited and there were errors that I missed when I self-published. I went completely down the rabbit hole concerning my competence and how the book would be viewed when I should have accepted my inexperience and not judged myself. Easier said than done. It cost me sleep and self-esteem and yet thrived in spite of my own ego deflation. Go figure.

Awareness and acceptance are always the keys, but how quickly we forget if it is *our* ego being bruised.

I have a book called *Living with Joy* by another spiritual teacher, Sanaya Roman that I have referred to often. One chapter is called "Refining the Ego—Recognizing who you are," and the author proposes in summary that we have made Power and Ego pretty much synonymous, but there are powerful people who are humble and perhaps they have learned the balance of being a good person and nurturing the ego at the same time. Roman says "Whatever you pay attention to is what you create." I can prove that with a silly example, when my hair began refusing to grow, specifically

A Life Winding Down

my bangs, I paid so much attention to it that my bangs did not grow for four months.

The most powerful influences in my life have been the gentle and positive people who refused to expound on how great they were. They just were. I envied that kind of acceptance of being in your own skin. My grandfather grew to be such a person. He was an avid reader of both Norman Vincent Peale and the Bible. He was happy to see you with a ready smile. He lived independently until he was 92. Sadly, he deteriorated in a nursing home, in a great deal of pain, but when you went to visit with him that positive spirit sat in a wheelchair with the Good Book in hand and smiled and was happy to see you. I have never forgotten that image. A visible soul inhabiting a failing body.

I will not name names, but you probably know several high-profile people of power who viciously attack others, verbally or physically, and who ruthlessly make decisions based on their greed and arrogance. Needless to say, their souls are not visible to us. In fact the Soul may have vacated and stays the distance. Hollow and soulless. Run as fast as you can!

If I have learned anything about the ego it is that it needs to be recognized as a part of our humanness, but that our true power is in our love, compassion, and gentle dignity. We will be remembered and honored for our goodness. So you say, Hitler is still remembered and he was none of the above. He has become a testament to the ego as a monster inside of us, but we also remember Mother Theresa, Jesus, Martin Luther King, Mandela, and Gandhi and millions more who exuded a selflessness that was far more influential.

We need not be immortalized for our acts of kindness and probably the above people would have preferred to do their work quietly, or we would be suspect that we acted out of ego and not from the heart. What is in a man's heart and soul may be most important to his impact on the world. In

Barbara Kemm-Highton

there somewhere the ego can play a role in the good or the evil that we project into the universe.

Be aware always of your intentions. Be aware of the ego.

Without treatment or engagement in recovery activities, addiction is progressive and can result in disability or premature death

(included in a definition by the American Society of Addictive Medicine)

ADDICTION

When I was trying to find an appropriate quote to address the horrors of addiction, I found, much like all of society, addiction is romanticized and often slyly supported, joked about, or becomes a badge to be worn by celebrity. Most everyone abuses drugs. If you think this is a lofty statement take a look at a perfectly legal set of drugs called alcohol and cigarettes. I know very few adults who do not have stories of their binge drinking, smoke filled high school and college days (myself included). The problem is that so many of my friends and drinking buddies are already dead or still abusing well into their elder years. In my family, alcohol and nicotine killed my uncle in his fifties and impaired my father until he passed away in his sixties.

Abusing chemicals in this country constitutes some unspoken right-of-passage. Parents accept that their kids are going to party and take illegal or legal substances and they assume that it is necessary and often turn a blind eye to the rampant abuse of their bodies and minds that is actually going on until there are some serious legal or medical consequences like DUIs, rapes, terrible car accidents or hospital stays for alcohol poisoning. After all, most adults themselves are frequently in bar situations, cookouts, country clubs, and family gatherings where the alcohol flows.

Kids follow other kids, but they also learn their behaviors from the family and some families teach their

Barbara Kemm-Highton

children that alcohol is an integral part of life and socializing. The problem is that most children go on to drink as college students and move on to happy hour as working adults, and then the cycle continues when these children become parents and teach their children that alcohol is an accepted part of family life. The picture is almost apple pie and *Leave it to Beaver* except addiction *is* the pink elephant in the room being ignored. A closer look shows that many of these families have had to deal with their own or their children's behaviors associated with drinking to excess. The family that encourages moderate alcohol on special occasions seems to be a very small percentage of our population.

I have been clean for 26 years and wish I had been so for all of my life. My drinking escalated from teen years to adult years and the chaos that addiction causes affected relationships, jobs, and my own children. I was 17 when I took note of my drinking and abuse of prescription drugs. I was in my 20s in the bar scene when I used cocaine for the first time. I was 30 when I was in rehab for "depression" an adjunct of mixing alcohol and sedatives. I was also unaware that I had suffered from a condition not yet commonly recognized, post partem depression. Sadly, three marriages and two children later, I was 45 when I was hospitalized after wrecking my car and was told that I needed alcohol treatment. I started attending AA two days later a chronological 45 year old performing as a 17 year old.

This could be anyone's story, but as I sat in daily meetings and heard the painful sagas of those in recovery, I realized that this is a national, at best, and global, at worst, dis-ease. I began to hear about the accidents, the people with multiple tickets, those who survived accidents and killed passengers, were drinking rubbing alcohol or cough medicines, lost jobs, lost spouses, children that were abandoned, children who died because of the parent's addictions, and this was just the tip of the iceberg.

A Life Winding Down

In the 1990s a survey of several major prisons in the US concluded that most convicted felons interviewed were drunk or high when they committed their crimes. These crimes ranged from car theft, burglary, and home invasion, to rape and murder. Of the interviewed group, many said they may not have committed the crime if they were not impaired, and many said they had blacked out and do not remember their crime at all.

An awful sidebar to being addicted means that when you are not present in the moment or impaired by chemicals, you can become essentially without a soul or without the power or compassion to make a healthy judgment about yourself or anyone else in your space. A large percentage of child beatings or deaths, wife beatings, and spousal attacks are people under the influence. Many home invasions and burglaries gone wrong involve someone who is high. A soulless body can commit a senseless murder, but we are not talking enough about this. Most of us, even those of us who abused chemicals recreationally, seem to be bewildered by these random acts. As a society, we should be seeing these connections, but we duck our heads and justify it by maintaining that when *we* get drunk *we* don't do this.

There is palpable damage to ourselves and our families when we become mentally impaired. Verbal abuses, embarrassment, and real physical harm can occur at any moment and this is why the whole family needs treatment for the addiction. Everyone is taken down by another family member's abuse of chemicals.

Turn on the television and tune in to the program *Intervention* to see the extreme cases of chronic addiction. The pain of the family almost comes through the television screen. Likely, if you have any feelings at all, you will squirm to hear how each person who shows up to help their loved one come to terms with the horrors of their dis-ease is emotionally spent, but most compelling is the life form that addiction spawns. The addicts are in pain but in such

Barbara Kemm-Highton

extreme denial that the person they once were has exited the body. They are dying before everyone's eyes and they have no power to stop.

If you walk away saying, "I am not *that* bad," you have missed the point. The point is, even mild abuse of alcohol and or drugs keeps a person from thinking clearly and presently in the moment. The consequences may pale by comparison to the hollow devastation of the hard-core addict, but small damages to your body and mind will add up. Make no mistake about this, alcohol consumed several times a week (even though all the heart and wine connection is now flaunted) does damage to your brain, heart and judgment skills.

I had known for many years before recovery that I was addicted. I liked to drink to relax, escape, feel better about myself, do what everyone was doing etc., etc., etc. My brain told me all of this. That insidious little voice in my head never said, "You are making your body and mind sick. Ethyl alcohol is a poison with the potential to kill brain cells." Even, "You will be throwing up your socks because you are poisoning yourself," might have given me pause.

If you are thinking for one minute that I am just jealous because I can't have a glass of wine with dinner once in a while, or I "couldn't hold my liquor" think again. I *could* hold **a lot** of liquor and that in itself was a problem. I am relieved that I no longer have to have alcohol, and, by the way I never had a glass of wine with dinner once in a while. Those people don't require treatment.

Alcohol is in the Bible is another excuse. If I am not mistaken drunkenness and gluttony is also.

May the forces of evil become confused on the way to your house.

George Carlin

EVIL

George Carlin was certainly comedic and not to be flip by using this phrase, I think he took evil as seriously as most of us do. The truth is, George, since you have passed on, I am guessing you have the answers now. The reality here on the Earth plane is that evil lurks and is rarely confused and *does* tragically make its way to many houses.

I have written about this topic before, but I fall short of understanding why a person becomes purely evil, so I will list all the things that I believe are evil and you can make your own such list and then I will attempt to let a few experts weigh in on the "whys."

The list of evil: It is not in order of importance. All of them are equally heinous.

1. Child killers, abusers or abductors. Personally, I believe they have no right to life since their recidivism rate is quite high.
2. Animal abusers (including all *slaughter* houses. I could care less about what the meat and poultry industry and all the sport hunters think about this). **Everything** created has the right to life and humane treatment.
3. Drug dealers and cartels specifically. Plain and simple. They kill souls as well as bodies. And I will group with them other pill pushers their ads, doctors and pharmacies that contribute to addictions and deaths.

Barbara Kemm-Highton

4. *Any* weapon because it destroys lives and the environment. Nuclear power is a disguise for the sinister.
5. Racism and discrimination
6. Religious cults and religious fanaticism.
7. Serial killers.
8. Any corporation mired in greed who is recklessly decimating the planet we live on. You know who you are. I can name names, but if your policy is profit at any cost then you are a mindless, soulless machine.
9. Any scientist, government or lab that experiments on humans and animals that results in monster-like hybrids, deaths, mind control, suicides etc. Do you really believe that the military in *this* country and the government has never participated in such acts? Think again! Google mind control experiments for starters.
10. Terrorists. Think Middle East, think school shooters, think any bombing including Oklahoma etc. Any person or persons who kills others to make a statement is evil. (I realize that many are mentally ill, so I will just recognize the actions as evil).
11. War (keep arguing that we have to have it and we most certainly will and we will wrap it in a flag and hand it an Uzi). Talk to any soldier about the crippling effects of their service and the evils they encountered, and make no mistake, they are heroes for sure, but we should be doing everything to promote peace so that they never have to come home so broken, or encased in a coffin, or never found again.
12. Doing nothing. Why? Because we allow evil to exist. When we participate in becoming silent about this then that very act allies us with that which we hate and fear.

A Life Winding Down

13. Political ads. We are outraged at bullying in general but we allow these defamations of character to be bought and played over and over again. Very Hitler like don't you think?
14. Online bullies and scammers, door to door scammers and phone scammers. So you think these people are not evil? Look at who they target— the elderly, children, and the mentally challenged. They are predators!
15. Pornography. Exploits, dehumanizes, causes addictions and worse it is a component of the glaringly sad disease of child pornography.
16. Children and teens being allowed to be cruel to each other with or without the internet. Bullies attack self-worth and self-esteem.
17. Sex slave trafficking of young children and adults. All involved should be eliminated. The death sentence is needed for them, in my opinion.
18. Anyone who rapes anyone or any animal (thanks in part to pornography). Date rapes are still a recurring news headline. Something I have experienced once in my life in college as have many other women I know.
19. Ruthless dictators.
20. Creating an economy based on the profits of the wealthy few while allowing others to starve and die. (If you think this is only Mexico or North Korea etc. might I remind you of the proliferation of homelessness, starvation, and disease that we pretend is their choice in **this** country).
21. Sweat shops and those who purchase from them.
22. Denying medical care to any human being. That would be the insurance companies, the government health plans, and in general the health care system. So why is *this* not considered murder?
23. Street drugs and some FDA approved drugs. They can cause addiction, death and violence. I say

Barbara Kemm-Highton

legalize only to take the cartels out of the equation but that does not eliminate addiction. I am almost more appalled by the legal drug deaths in this country by companies that manufacture them for outrageous profit. Just say "No" and the "War on Drugs" has had very limited success. The opiate addiction flourishes as I write.

I have no expertise when it comes to identifying or explaining evil, so I will refer you to some of the books that I have randomly read and let you decide.

In, *The Science of Evil: On Empathy and the Origins of Evil,* Cambridge professor Simon Baron-Cohen, takes a clinical look at some of the labeled in society and how they perform, i.e., sociopaths, psychopaths, narcissists and borderline personality disorders. Scientifically speaking, there are parts of their brain that have damaged electrical currents thus empathy or remorse cannot be manifested.

Cohen contends that some patients as young as 4 who cannot process right from wrong may be in danger of becoming an antisocial personality disorder, and that punishment seems to have little effect.

Causally speaking, abuse or neglect, trauma to the brain and stress can also damage these vital currents and make someone dangerous to others. According to the experts, genetics is a very slippery slope, so it is not always a deciding factor in a diagnosis.

Some of the characteristics that contribute to a dangerous personality type are: aggression, a sense of entitlement, abuse, neglect, anger, lack of empathy and narcissism. There also seems to be some connection to profound depression in an individual. For example, Cohen says in the well-known Columbine school shootings, a teacher of one of shooters, described him as depressed and suicidal leaving him temporarily brain damaged while the other appeared to be the ongoing psychopathic personality since he had allegedly made statements that the victims were

A Life Winding Down

"stupid people who needed to be killed." It is Cohen's belief that we should be trying to rehabilitate even the minute good we can find in these subjects.

We can debate this all day long, and I do believe we should reconsider the fate of those prisoners who have found true remorse and are trying to help others from prison. Many of them are executed while there was Charles Manson, damaged to the core, even if it was an act, who orchestrated many murders that tax payers had been burdened with housing since the '70s. My opinion is that he was not a productive prisoner and maintained a cult even from his cell, but then I have no comprehension of his journey or why he was here. He finally received an exit door when he passed away last year and then he was further immortalized by a documentary or two, headlines about his estate and recognition of his loyal followers who were mourning his death. We are responsible for this morbid fascination with the evil infamous.

Cohen believes we need more resources to reach the anti-socials before they become these infamous killers. No argument there and I should add, this isn't going away because we throw money elsewhere and it hasn't happened to us. If your loved one is murdered by one of these societal defectives then you understand, and all of us should know it could be any person's loved one. Make it your problem too. Demand those resources.

We are also a society of women who sometimes choose to marry an antisocial male with serious consequences to our life and the lives of our children and pets. The psychiatrist's bible, the DSM IV, in summary describes the antisocial as usually a person who abuses others and animals. They are vandals who did not do well in school. They lie and cheat and steal and commit serious rule violations and did so as small children. They are alcohol and drug abusers. They can commit a crime without a conscience.

Barbara Kemm-Highton

According to Doctor Donald W. Black in *Bad Boys, Bad Men,* antisocials act on impulse and are reckless with cars even with you and your children in them. They get into fights and cannot hold down a job. They are often engaged in illegal activities and can do so with impunity because they lack remorse. Black also contends that even with these distinctive markers, they are often elusive to diagnose even for the experts. Labeling juveniles is often discouraged, so they may be full blown adults living with someone and their vulnerable children before they can be recognized as these scary misfits. Not all of them kill, but some do and some intimidate in ways that are incomprehensible like shooting the family pet in front of the children.

This type of soulless disorder is not changeable. Most certainly not by some hapless man or woman who has chosen this personality for a spouse, and even if the experts may disagree, there are some of these people who are not able to be rehabilitated.

Are there then just dark entities inhabiting a body? Whatever the reason is that they are soulless, it needs our vigilant attention. If this can be averted by nurturing and loving in infancy and childhood, then we should be providing this for *every* child on the planet.

If you are in a relationship with an adult antisocial who is abusing you and your children, then you have no power to help. Run! Save yourself and your children.

If a person without remorse is already operating as an adult, it is unlikely he or she will seek help. Without any filters needed to discern right from wrong they are incapable of seeking help according to definition.

If your loved one is killed by a serial killer, they are not capable of remorse. I get why families want an apology for a random killing, (and sometimes they do say "I am sorry"), but in all likelihood what you are asking is for them to grow a conscience when they have no ability to do so.

A Life Winding Down

When an Illinois serial killer was interviewed about his victims, he conceded that he was sure that if he wasn't locked up, he would kill again. Many such prolific killers have affirmed that they do not know why they killed, but they would do it again. Chilling, but as honest as they can be.

By the way, many serial killers look for their victims alone on the street. That means prostitutes, hitchhikers, and drunken partiers are often the easy targets of these hunters.

I don't believe in the devil per se, but I do believe that evil exists and can reside in a human body. We have that proof in child killers, school shooters, terrorists and other monsters in society. We need to care about changing the circumstances of all the babies that are born so they are less likely to grow up to become killers, at worst, or just psychologically damaged in general. If evil can be stopped before it develops then why would we not try?

The greatness of a nation and its moral progress can be judged by the way its animals are treated.
                                    Mahatma Gandhi

ANIMALS

When I was a child, I loved horses, but at 5 years old, I was less than cordial to our family pet. I teased and chased and terrorized my dog and that makes me very ashamed of myself since I am an animal advocate and animal lover today.

I have often pondered why my parents did not admonish this behavior, and I have come to the conclusion that they liked the family pet, but basically had little connection to its spiritual nature. Animals come and go so to speak. Without a leash law our dog ran the streets and disappeared for whole days. This apathy has changed over the years and many of us consider our pets a huge part of the family, not to mention leash laws and better care have extended their time with us on the Earth plane. Our dog, Boots, was resilient and wise and lived to be 15 years old with minimal vet visits since we had very little money to spend. When my mother asked me to make the call to have Boots put down for a heart condition (she could not), it was one of the hardest things I had had to do at 19 years old. I have since had to make that decision several times. It doesn't get any easier.

It is becoming more apparent in society that animals can be service animals, military heroes, therapists, and in some cases better physicians since many can detect diseases that have not been diagnosed. Their intelligence and their refined senses are being respected by more and more organizations and the fight to save their lives and preserve the gift to us that they are have become a global concern.

Animals are majestic, loyal, loving and keenly intelligent. However, many are often treated as disposable.

Barbara Kemm-Highton

They are abused, abandoned, maimed and killed for sport. Their babies are dumped on highways to be run over or left in abandoned homes to starve to death. Endangered species are hunted and killed for their horns, paws, and heads. Slaughter animals are over produced, over fed, inhumanely butchered and living in painful conditions prior to their killings to be served in fast food restaurants to our babies. Slaughter and butcher are titles of some of these buildings and occupations. Let that digest for a moment!

My hat is off to PETA, the ASPCA, Betty White, Doris Day, the late Mrs. Bob Barker, the Humane Societies and No Kill Shelters, Animal Control workers, Sara Mclachlan, Wendie Malick , Jane Goodall, and Kathryn Bigelow and millions of other animal rights activists, but we need to do much more to prevent the over population of unwanted animals.

If I anger these people: all sport hunters especially big game hunters who kill endangered animals, farmers that engage in abusive, exploitive cruelty, gangsters who keep exotic animals in their basements, dog-nappers who extort money for their return, dog-nappers who sell them to be eaten in other countries, juveniles who torture and kill animals, any adult or child who abuses or kills animals (you might become a serial killer, by the way), anyone who has too many animals and leaves them to starve, puppy mill operators, and those who exploit and bet on animals forced to fight to the death (remember Michael Vick? although he may have reformed his ways) then I have done my job.

I will let our creator be tolerant and forgiving of these people. I don't have it in me. They prove to me that we have no conscience and we have not evolved. They disgust me.

This chapter is dedicated to Tweety, Boots, Clyde, Bo, Zeb, Charlotte, Kayba and Drooper on the other side and for the unconditional love we share with our dogs Fred and Luna today.

Whoever controls the media, controls the mind.
                                                   Jim Morrison

MEDIA AND ENTERTAINMENT

Hopefully, today's, Jim Morrison, the former lead singer of The Doors, would be appalled to see his drug and alcohol fueled stage antics on an endless YouTube loop. Had he not died of his abuses, he would possibly see his prophetic quote being proved and tested on every hand-held device imaginable. I envision a years sober and clean artist and poet being horrified by the mindless control that has now become "The Media."

I really *like* television but *love* a good book (a real one not on a hand-held) and as a teacher and writer I love my iPad and iPhone, but I am mystified by all the blogs and tweets and comments and hatred spewed across their screens. I do not Tweet and find this kind of obsessive following of others frightening. The door to abuse is open wide. This of course is not new news so let's break down the good the bad and the downright ugly!

I am going to try to sound like I am not 105 years-old here. I grew up with a black and white TV in my home. It had to be monitored very little because I would rather be outside on my bike or at the pool or the library,

In the '50s I would have been a grade schooler and although I saw a few programs like *I Love Lucy*, *The Ed Sullivan Show*, *Lassie* and *Leave it to Beaver,* I remember thinking this was not like most families and corny and often the adult humor of other shows escaped me. I understood the open drinking on *The Jackie Gleason Show,* (a favorite of my parents).

Barbara Kemm-Highton

Toward the '60s, it was the era of the westerns. I like them now as nostalgia, but then and now I was appalled at the portrayal of the Indians and the animals. Like most tween and teen girls I fell in love with Michael Landon, Steve McQueen and admired James Arness. Oddly, I was a fan of Richard Boone and his rugged but educated demeanor in *Have Gun Will Travel*.

High school social life ate up 4 years of mindless cheerleading, underage drinking parties, dances and cruising (a little school as well). I don't remember watching a single show then except maybe *The Twilight Zone*. I still preferred reading. I was a huge Victoria Holt mysteries fan. I also read *Catcher in the Rye*. It was required in the austere and punitive environment that was a Catholic school in the 1960s. Go figure.

From there TV became sitcoms and detective shows. Leading men in bell bottoms with side burns trying to emulate black street lingo is still humorous today and as cheesy. As a young mother in the '70s and trying to hold down a fulltime teaching job, I would drink in front of the TV, but I remember little impact from the scripted fare, but I vividly remember the news. It had changed from the carefully edited black and white, singly anchored, monotone reporters to the searing scenes of the Vietnam War from the brave reporters and camerapersons who brought us the truth of the horrors in another zone. The movie *Apocalypse Now* stayed with me for years, as well.

I will skip the '80s and early '90s since I think I actually did.

Today I have rather eclectic tastes in television, but have little interest in listening to people whine about each other over cocktails. That said I can't even pay attention to all the silly housewives. Why are we throwing money at people who are demeaning themselves and their families? I know the answer. We are a society that feels good about watching others behave badly or babble on about where to spend their

A Life Winding Down

money next. I am so uncomfortable watching people exploit themselves for money and exposure (in more ways than one). How many people need to see a person's large tanned butt? Never mind, a lot of people do.

I like Netflix, *Copper,* (which was excellent and cancelled) and I like a montage of other original series, *The Killing, Marcella, and Travelers* among them. Some of these have also disappeared.

On the regular TV side I am a fan of *Cold Justice, Younger, Real Time With Bill Maher, Dateline, 48 Hours (Longmire, The Bridge,* and *The Killing* all cancelled, but excellently written and performed and renewed on Netflix), *60 Minutes, PBS News Hour, the* antithesis of *Fox News, Justified,* (series ended, not sure why), *Ray Donovan, Divorce, Last Week Tonight With John Oliver, The Killing Fields, The Middle, and Modern Family.*

I love my hand-held devices and texting my granddaughter. I am reluctantly on Facebook and was soon angry at the multitude of anti-Obama posts that I was being sent. Oh, and I am angry about the recent debacle of all of us being allegedly targeted by the injection of fake news and the sharing of our information to become further targeted. We should have known.

We all appear to be racist, religious fanatics and I am reasonably sure that these two adjectives should never be together. I am ashamed of us on blogs and tweets and Facebook showing our grotesque hatred of others. We need to fight this invasion of social media by evil forces no matter who they are. This ability to be a monster hidden in cyberspace is something we should never have become and should have predicted. There were those who knew an adversary would spread false news and divide a democracy. Now we all know!

Moving on from the racism and bullying that goes on non-stop, I am also alarmed by the porn, sex trafficking, violence, internet predators, scammers, and identity thieves

Barbara Kemm-Highton

and hackers that are literally part of our daily clicking lives. My hat is off to all the behind the scenes professionals who are trying to close the door even an inch, but we have literally leapt forward in technology without a safety net.

If Atlantis was truly an advanced society that disappeared, did they too create a monster of technology who ultimately stopped their spiritual evolution and annihilated their race? It is something to think about.

> *Millions of spiritual creatures walk the earth unseen,*
> *both when we wake and when we sleep.*
> John Milton, *Paradise Lost*

ANGELS

Ethereal, mostly pictured winged, magical beings of light are the subject of art work both ancient and modern, but what are they really?

In my research, at least, they appear to be something otherworldly that manifests when we need guidance or during horrible times of duress, an accident, a force of nature, or during an NDE. They appear in the texts of sacred books around the world, the Bible, the Book of Enoch, the Qur'ran and others. They have also been photographed or at the very least have shown up on the digital images of many an unsuspecting photographer. (Look up some of these pictures. I realize today that photo-shopping has muddied these waters). On the religious side, many prophets including Muhammad, Abraham, Moses and Joseph Smith have all claimed to have been influenced by such a visitation. They have been recounted in many books about near death experiences, war time battlefield encounters, and many psychics claim their existence.

Christianity proposes that an angel appeared to the blessed Mary to inform her of the virgin birth that is crucial to that faith, and I am not at all here to diminish any of these experiences.

I seem to have some connection to the angel Ariel. When I did a little more reading on the subject, I was struck by the association this particular guide has to nature and to my astrological sign. Ariel seems to be the angel most connected to the animals and the environment which are dear to me as well. A side note is that I found a book several years

Barbara Kemm-Highton

ago read it and set it aside. I pulled it off the shelf as a reference when I started this chapter. It is called, *Interview with An Angel* by Steven Thayer and Linda Sue Nathanson. Thayer was an electrical engineer with a Masters' degree in the field, until he had a mystical experience involving an angel and then developed a therapy system of counseling called IET that combines touch based energy and spirituality for healing. Nathanson PhD is the founder of The Edin Group, Inc. and is an educated research psychologist.

I began to reread their text that appears to be channeled through Thayer by an angel. Are you ready? I was a little surprised myself. That angel being asked all the questions possible by these authors is Ariel! I don't believe in coincidences much, but you can write it off as that if you so choose.

Switching gears now let's look at a whole new avenue of explanation. Another book that has intrigued me is *We've Never Been Alone* by Paul Von Ward. Von Ward has a most impressive resume. He is a Mensa member, an ordained minister and psychologist who also served for 30 years as a Navy officer, US. diplomat, and international educator.

The following quote is from his book jacket "Call them gods, angels, ETs, or spirit entities—beings more advanced than humans have shaped our history. They shaped our religions, our genes, our technology, and our cultures. In fact, it appears that they provided the impetus for modern civilization."

Von Ward is highly intelligent and an avid researcher. He does address all the major religions and their first conception of the gods. His term for the angels or gods is the ABs or "advanced beings." I will let each reader who chooses his book delve into the meticulous presentation of the many documented sources of proof of the ABs in every ancient culture in all corners of the globe. Suffice it to say, this scholar maintains that the conversations need to be had by every human being and the veil of secrecy and mis-

A Life Winding Down

information needs to be lifted so that we can freely communicate with the origin of our species whether that be messengers of a god, or planetary beings that may have seeded us and continue to try to guide and inform the varied species they have introduced. By the way, even if we were seeded by other alien races, in many of the encounters humans have claimed to have had with the aliens or ABs the information they shared was often about trying to encourage mankind to become more spiritual.

So if the ABs/angels/aliens represent a Supreme Being (Mother/Father/ Creator) their prevailing message appears to be one of a peaceful co-existence such as they have attained and this is the path to a universal Source and access to the higher vibrational realms. But, as a race, we seem to be ignoring these messengers or watchers and we have descended into chaos in many places on this planet.

So what is afoot here? Almost all angel/alien visions have had a profound influence on the receiver to become a healer or to lead a life of recognizing the beauty of the world and our connectedness to every living thing. Edgar Cayce was told in a vision delivered by what he called an angel that he would be able to do something special to help mankind. Since he was just a child at the time, he would not know that the "something" would be his ability to be a trance medium. He would be able to answer questions about natural healing which would then be documented into the many volumes we still access today. While he was in this sleep state, he would also be privy to all of the answers to the world's greatest unsolved mysteries including the building of the pyramids. He revealed that we once had the powers of levitation.

So, if these alien ancestors, guides, ascended masters, or angels keep revealing themselves to us to assist us with a higher frequency of love and God's transcendence, why are we embroiled in hatred and separateness and killing in the name of a god?

Barbara Kemm-Highton

Are there perhaps influences here that scramble our communications for power, greed and control? According to many ufologists, mediums and healers, about 5 percent of the extraterrestrial contact is based on evil and mind-control, but what then is our protection? If we think we are asking the angels or Mother and Father God for help or assistance are we letting in the monsters? My guess is that the monsters among us are dark entities and I personally ask Ariel specifically and the light Source to keep me in a safe light. Many mediums adhere to this practice as well. If we all asked to stand in the white or golden light and were open to help, be it our good alien protectors or God's messengers, would we be transformed? I like to think so, and it should be a global movement.

If there are angels and demons or good and bad extraterrestrials then who are the majority of us talking to? I would say the governments of most countries know and all the mega religions know as well, but it has been withheld for control purposes and because most of us are on auto pilot we are not questioning anything.

It can't hurt to get to know your friendly neighborhood angel/alien.

I can be changed by what happens to me, but I refuse to be reduced by it.

Maya Angelou

SEXUAL ASSAULT OR HARASSMENT

#METOO became the movement and even though during the campaign of 2016 the women accusing the candidate were largely ignored, it took one movie mogul to cause the dominos to fall. Perhaps it doesn't matter the catalyst but the deafening silence that has been the backdrop of society for centuries became a clamoring. There was vocal support and then swift action. We who have been assaulted were liberated. We could come out of the shadows and tell the secrets.

Here are mine. I was stalked by a man when I was 18. He terrified me in my parents' home with menacing phone calls. He followed me from my job to school. He was a bus driver; a grown man. I confronted him one day when I spotted him outside my workplace. I was fortunate that my stalker was benign, and a serial killer named Ted Bundy would come much later. One down and I had a voice. I felt empowered, but only for a moment.

Insecure and young, I accepted a blind date with a mentally disturbed man who had been making obscene phone calls to me prior to the arranged date. I had no idea they were one and the same person. After a barn party and some alcohol, we all started a hay fight. When my date was hit in the face, he suddenly pounced on me and began choking me. If I had been alone with him I am not sure that he would have let me live. I was shaken but enlightened. Or so I thought.

Barbara Kemm-Highton

I worked long hours to pay for college and could not afford to belong to a sorority any longer, so I entered the lonely life of being a free agent on the campus. I was just a working student. Dating was sparse and when I went anywhere it was to party. The drinking was an integral part of college life and for me the beginning of an addiction that I would wrestle with for many more years. While it is a cautionary tale to warn women about the dangers of being incapacitated around males, it is also not an excuse to be used for predation.

A transfer student, a football player, a frat boy, one of the people who *belonged* asked me out after a few casual meetings. He was quiet and brooding. I mistook this for shyness. I was 19 and graduate of a small Catholic school. For all my socializing, I had had only one other sexual experience. This rape was an assault born of power and hatred. I was instantly sobered and adamantly protested. I said "No" and that was the impetus for me to be raped in his car, covered in my own menstrual blood and thrown out of the car to walk home at 2 a.m. I was stunned. I walked to my parents' home with a zombie-like buzzing in my head. I showered and showered and placed my clothes in the bottom of our burn barrel. I remembered the few girls who had timidly stepped up to accuse a rapist in the culture of the late '60s. Their names were in the newspaper and they were discredited. Other men stepped up to testify to how loose they were.

My father had probably not meant this to apply to sexual assault, but he preached that if anything happened to me while I was drinking, it was my fault. My mother was embarrassed that I had been caught drinking under age and my name had been in the paper. It made her look bad at her job.

So the silence began. It was the only choice. I was nobody. I wouldn't win, and I would be humiliated. It needed to be buried deeply.

A Life Winding Down

But it seeps into all aspects of your life. I became a divorced mother. I drank too much. I had low self-esteem. I was with two men who used alcohol and drugs and they were abusive. I lost my way and I lost my soul. I had talked only twice after the attack. One was to a random girl standing in line to register for classes. I was so distraught that my perp was in line ahead of me that I confessed to a stranger. She said he had done the same thing to her friend. What are the odds? Then during treatment for post partem depression, a psychiatrist asked about any traumas in my life and I said, "Oh, yeah, I was date raped."

It was an out of body experience and it was on the table. Later I sealed the envelope and put it in the back of the drawer.

I am a grandmother now with two beautiful granddaughters. One is an adult and she knows the story. The other is too little, but I worry about how women are still treated. This is for both of them.

Never believe that you need to be ashamed of your gender. Men are not superior to women. Never be silent and always know that you can be a victim if you lose awareness. There are good, loving men out there and they will respect and honor you and protect you. They never own, control or abuse you. They never try to make you believe you are unworthy. You are strong, beautiful and smart. You are a pure untouched spirit.

It was all over the news. Every night it seemed another man (I have not forgotten the assaulted men) or woman stepped up, but very slowly embedded in the voices was a simmering distrust. Men and women began to question all the injustices that were being aired. An alleged pedophile was defended and supported for a Senate seat. People went on television to call the women, many were children younger than I had been, liars. The many strides forward were several steps backward. And then there were some accusations that were categorized as harassment, but not physical assault, and

Barbara Kemm-Highton

the hairs began to split. Jobs were being removed for inappropriate conversations with women. (I am not defending this either since I have been victimized by this as well) but the rules became all or nothing. This gave the naysayers fuel to lump all the men and women coming forward as hysterical and out to get any man who had made an off-color remark. Then the celebrities caused a groundswell again and spoke in solidarity, and we felt we had an inspired voice. The tide of support laps the shore and then is taken back out to sea. All civil rights have evolved and all civil rights have grown exponentially only to be discredited by the evil inherent in discrimination.

The current President denies his sexual accusers. Others accused are calling all of them consensual even when the numbers are staggering and the stories the same.

For those of us denied the right to tell the truth, I believe that as MLK, a bible follower, said so eloquently at a visit to the nearly all white Grosse Pointe South High School in Detroit, "I still believe that freedom is the bonus you receive for telling the truth. Ye shall know the truth and the truth shall set you free." And that my fellow travelers *is* The Truth.

Earth provides enough to satisfy every man's needs, but not every man's greed.

Mahatma Gandhi

EARTH

Outside of bumping into things and large amounts of gasses and dusts and explosions, the formation of the planet known as Earth is mired in theory, mystery, and complex mathematical equations. Not to discredit the elite and intelligent persons promoting their theories, we still do not have a timeline (other than theory) that gives us the knowledge of the origins of the planet that we have inhabited for millions of years. Or have we?

Speculatively, the earth formed in an eon that is translated into Hades (the underworld from Greek mythology). Odd! Nudging, flying particles and volcanic eruptions aside, all of this answered little since the earth somehow came into being fully equipped with the best ever feature of a product—oceans. And this is not the only head scratcher for anyone who has ever mused: How did we get here and where did we come from? It is when we cannot account for the varied races of humans that appeared not long after (according to the textbooks) amoebas and dinosaurs.

So, along comes religion and the Bible throwing logic out the window. We all came from a single man and woman. Thus, to this day you have many people who discount the findings of human fossils that are millions of years old, since they do not support the biblical story of the Garden of Eden. I am certain that teaching your children that dinosaurs did not exist and nothing else did until the creation portrayed in the Bible is made more difficult by the vast numbers of fossil

Barbara Kemm-Highton

recreations that are viewed in museums in all corners of the world.

In all things Earth, it is imperative that we keep that precious gift of an *open* mind. I have but to look at the beauty and mystery of the planet I live on to realize there is more at work here than some happenstance of colliding debris. I also realize that more needs to be proffered concerning ancient civilizations. If we dig really deep into the inhabitants of the globe, there seems to be more than a few gaps in the physical traits of certain populations existing in certain regions according to the dating technologies we currently employ. In other words, if we came from one man and one woman how did we become so diversified. And isn't this theory, one man and one woman, promoting both cloning *and* incest?

My guess is that we were created elsewhere and then plopped on this planet. Does this then eliminate the concept of a creator or a god? I have read a butt load of New Age material including many on the subject of alien encounters. The vast majority (excluding the evil alien encounters) recount that the message they were given is that humanity must connect to God and that they themselves are more spiritually evolved and that our lack of peace and our greed and decimation of the planet proves how low we are on the spiritual ladder so to speak.

The pleas to save this planet have been coming for centuries. Perhaps it is irrelevant how we came into being, and it is much more important to figure out how to save the gift that was given to us: Life on Earth.

Nostradamus has been much studied about his forewarnings concerning the demise of our world. Shrouded in secrecy and practicing an art of sorcery as it was seen, he risked his life to tell us we must take action to avoid disasters. He was alive in the 1500s. Edgar Cayce and the Bible for that matter have been touting "the end of days."

A Life Winding Down

The late scientist Stephen Hawking said we need to be in space to find another inhabitable planet. Not prone to conspiracy theories or alien interventions this icon of intelligence who had battled the disease of ALS for 50 years, was warning humanity that we cannot hope to sustain this planet at the current rate of pollution that we have accepted.

I am struck by the rhetoric that plays out in the local news, and I wonder just how evil the machinery for profit must be. Carbon emissions are being blamed for much of the destruction of clean air and the Obama administration had been trying to at least lesson the damage. That was obliterated by the current party in power. A utility spokesperson warns of loss of jobs and higher utilities and cites the lessoning of carbon emissions when *all* carbon emissions are dangerous to our health as is the storing of coal dust. (It is the same argument by the addicted smoker to only have one cigarette a day when smoking is the leading cause of lung cancer). Are utility companies just asleep at the wheel? Are they negligent or misled and I want to know why more jobs are not being created by renewable resources? I know the answer is money, but at what cost? Our life span, our breathable air and a safer planet are being determined by employing people who continue to contaminate the planet and then defend the contamination.

I see most of us globally as complacent if not complicit in the game of death by human consumption. We are allowing rich corporations to destroy the oceans. We are looking the other way when governments test nuclear weapons *in the ocean*. We are believing the many politicians who are trying to avoid the issues of global warming or climate change or whatever you want to call it because they want their political aspirations to be funded by the same machinery that allows the planet to be contaminated! Do I seem like I am screaming? I am. I have children and grandchildren. I do not want them to die from lack of food, water, or air. These were all gifts that we have plundered like

Barbara Kemm-Highton

barbarian soldiers because we think what? Do we think we can do nothing? Do we think that as a group conscience we could not stop this? That my friends is complacency at its worst and victims by choice.

I will give you some examples that demanding change can make things happen. When enough people are determined to stop atrocities (think the march at Selma) then change happens. When the priest abuse scandals came to light, things changed. When police departments were scrutinized for their racial profiling some things changed.

Here is a hypothetical. If we all stopped voting for any candidate of any party who is in the pocket of rich supporters like big banks, oil companies, pharmaceutical companies, factory giants, or insurance companies, it would change. (Slippery slope because the spin doctors get to the voters and essentially lie so that the candidate looks like a good Christian who abhors abortion while allowing these companies to kill our existing babies!) You think I am lying? Do some legitimate reading or credible internet searching.

I swear, I am not just picking on the Catholic church, unfortunately, it is the only one I was an insider of. If all the good Catholics said wait a minute; I think I will just leave this religion a) because they do not allow women positions in the church and b) because the Vatican bank has allegedly been laundering money for the Mob or c) because they discriminate against gays, the divorced, and women who have had abortions.

If all the parishioners (money and attendance) left, I guarantee these things would change. All of them could agree to come back on one condition. All the church's secrets would be transparent, and these antiquated laws reversed. I know this might not happen because many people are blinded by faith and most of them agree with a and c. They might take issue with b but do not believe it is true.

Back to the Earth. Which I never really left but might be forced to some day. Much has been written about the Earth

A Life Winding Down

and I am not an expert, I am an inhabitant who would like to see us preserve our future.

    I was recently called a "tree hugger" by someone who apparently is not in need of oxygen. I do not find it offensive, and I am shocked that anyone would think that over logging, any excessive deforesting projects etc. would not be considered detrimental to our lives. If we lose the air we breathe and our ecosystems, we are gone. It is pretty simple, so I will be a tree, ocean, animal, land hugger until I take my last breath which may be coming faster than I want it to.

The truth will set you free, but first it will piss you off.
Joe Klass

"AMERICA LAND OF THE FREE"

I am going to have to argue the point. Put the flag down and the Bible and while you are at it the textbooks. We have been sold a bill of goods. We are deceived into believing that we truly are free. By comparison to other countries we have freedom of speech and religion, and I am eternally grateful to have these basic freedoms although the trade-offs concern me and the abuse of these freedoms do as well.

Let's take a much closer look at what is enslaving the country.

1. Oil and oil companies. I encourage you to read the book *Crude Justice* by Stuart H. Smith. Chevron, Exxon and BP have been sued for their reckless decimation and pollution and, yes, the deaths of many of the workers in the Gulf region parts of which are called Cancer Alley. They have allegedly exposed people and their families to toxic waste and contamination of the ocean, soil and water and allegedly they knew they were doing this all along. If you think the Gulf is back to normal because of the PR ads, think again.
2. Evil corporations. The list is too long. It is capitalism without a conscience. They are our masters. They control all the money. Yes, they are banks and mortgage companies. Look at where they took us just recently.

They control the pesticides and contaminations that enter the food supplies. They make our defective cars with air bags that can kill us with shrapnel.

Barbara Kemm-Highton

When we complain, the response is almost always that we will be costing money to change a system and the one that always gets us—JOBS!

3. Pharmaceutical Companies and their co-conspirators Insurance Companies. We need life saving drugs, but many are dangerous and kept on the market for profit when they are actually killing the patients. The price of some drugs are being inflated that have been around for decades. These corporations fund campaigns and lobby to keep the machinery going. Their products are overprescribed and their markets are about profit. How could this go wrong? If we were free we would have choices in this arena. We do not. We are held hostage by the need for a drug and the insurance companies who can either refuse to cover it therefore making it out of reach or accept the inflated pricing. As a disclaimer, I realize that many companies are trying to fund needed medicines for the poor and elderly. This is commendable, but let's get to the root of the problem. Lots and lots of research continues and strides are being made, but one example is despite the money and time and effort and the promising research, we are still killing cancer patients with chemo no matter how much money has been thrown at the disease. It does work for some but it is a crap-shoot for who will die or develop other illnesses from basically being poisoned. There are trials and encouraging new treatments that move very slowly at the mercy of the FDA, and let's face it, cancer is a profitable illness. Need I say more?

We are also a flagrantly overmedicated country. The only entity benefitting from this legal addiction is the drug maker and perhaps the doctors promoting and using their products.

Finally, please watch the documentary *Fire in the Blood*. Western drug companies and governments

A Life Winding Down

allegedly denied lifesaving generic AIDs drugs to Africa and other globally poor countries. Many people are quoted and the consensus is basically: If you fight the patent laws which decide and control affordable drugs, you will be left to die! They allegedly engaged in murder to protect profits according to the heartbreaking film narrated by actor William Hurt with cameos by Bill Clinton, George W. Bush, Nelson Mandela, and Bishop Desmond Tutu. It will change your opinion of Western Pharma and some of the executives that run these companies.

To all the doctors without borders, all the hospitals and doctors who are tending to the poor, you are the true heroes. The rest of the system often seems to be less about patient care and more about need versus greed. That is a form of slavery.

4. Technology. It is both a blessing and a curse, but look around you. Millions of people are on hand held devices day and night, while driving and eating. We are not engaging in human contact and unwilling to stop texting while driving even though we are killing others. This is enslavement. My sons commented that while they were in Europe they did not see people on cell phones all day. They were walking, eating, and talking to each other on a personal level. We are enslaved by and addicted to battery powered machines!

5. For profit mega churches. People are tithing and paying for expensive buildings and pastors are strutting around with mics like boy-banders on a big screen to promote more and more people to pay for the blessings of God, oh, and to pay for the houses and cars of the pastors, some of them in the elite range price-wise. This seems like total nonsense to me, but for the enraptured flock this seems okay. This is enslavement of the emotionally needy who want

Barbara Kemm-Highton

desperately to buy their way into heaven and make an ordinary (and now wealthy) man or woman a conduit to the Divine.
6. Guns. I can see a huge sea of men in pickup trucks and their wives and kids all in camo gear spit stomping mad and the NRA president becoming red faced and indignant (he can rant and rave since this is the most powerful organization of lobbyists known to man). We have taken the second amendment to a degree probably not intended. We have a total disregard for any kind of control even though it is killing children and destroying families. We do not want anyone kept from weapons even the mentally ill. It makes us a slave to the weapon. In states and countries where there is control the stats prove that it works to stem the violence, but we are backing down from the NRA even after all the Sandy Hook, Columbine, and Parkland parents and students asked for more background checks and sensible gun control. The only beacon of hope is the student marchers who are promising to rid Congress of the NRA butt kissers by exercising their voting rights. Until then we are enslaved by arming ourselves.
7. History. Do we have it right? There are many archeologist, paleontologists, forensic anthropologists, historians and other credentialed scholars who are saying: Wait a minute! We are finding anomalies in the research. Please read *Our Occulted History* by the late Jim Marrs or watch *Ancient Aliens*. I will only say that many of these people are questioning what has been placed in our history books. It is well known that Columbus was not the first to set foot on the Americas. (This doesn't stop the day off and the silly parades, however). In fact, there is odd evidence found in caves that perhaps the Egyptians and the Incas were here well before that. There are ancient

A Life Winding Down

maps of the area that are head scratchers. There have allegedly been skulls found that when tested were not human DNA. Allegedly, a race of giants was unearthed but the museum that supposedly received the bones denies having them. Are we then enslaved by misinformation? Are we being kept from knowing who we are and where we really came from?

8. Prisons. Many are for profit. Prisons are overcrowded and sentences are harsh even for marijuana charges. The enslaved are overwhelmingly minorities. If you have the money to pay expensive lawyers, you may do less time than the poor. This is enslavement at every level. Then the enslaved have no jobs or dignity or skills when they are released only to return to the penal system. (Side note: Many are being released to ease the overcrowding, but they are being given few options for a better life.) The freed slaves faced a similar dilemma.

9. Human trafficking and or Sex slavery. It goes without saying that this is the most despicable act on the planet—the buying and selling of young women and children and forcing them into prostitution and or pornography. It is not just here but other countries, but we cannot look away. We have buyers and sellers in this country who are okay with exploiting and selling human beings for sex. Many are as young as 2.

   Human refugees are also being smuggled in and left to die while trying to enter countries to escape poverty, war, abuse, and starvation. It is also murder to leave them locked in trucks without food, water, or air. Why are the traffickers not in prison or, sorry, executed?

10. Drugs. We are an illegally and legally medicated country. We have alcohol, we have prescription drugs, and we have all the illegal drugs. We are

Barbara Kemm-Highton

actually providing cartels and gangs with the ability to commit violent crimes. We keep them in business via our addictions.

I am a recovering addict, so I do know the lifestyle and the disease. After more than two decades clean and no desire to escape the world or drown my problems by getting high, I firmly believe we legalize at least marijuana and perhaps other drugs. All the Evangelicals will balk, but they probably are not using street drugs. Stop the ruthless murders associated with cartels and gangs by removing their products. I know this is simplistic, but we don't seem to be able to prevent people from getting high and it is killing our children—still. We are the market for these drugs. Many countries do not allow the rampant abuse that goes on here. I realize there will still be addicts. They should have more assistance with recovery anyway. Throw the money there not to some cartel that is dipping humans in vats of acid as retaliation in drug wars. We fund and create these monsters. Where do you think your drugs come from? Your Meth likely comes from a house where babies may be crawling on the floor while the parents are cooking chemicals that can explode. You are paying for this!

11. Gender. Women are still subjected to violence and death worldwide. Domestic violence is part of our western culture. Women still do not always receive equal pay or promotions. Many women are not allowed positions in churches. Most of the people killed by serial killers are women. Many women are still questioned and not always believed in a sexual assault case. Thus, the reluctance to pursue.

We think because we are in this country that we have more freedoms and by comparison we are allowed to show our faces, drive cars, report rapes,

A Life Winding Down

marry whom we choose and have health care options (including abortion which one party is trying to take away as I write). The other side of the coin is that we are still covertly discriminated against in many areas of our lives, and watch any crime show and you will realize that the percentage of spouses killed is highest among women.

For the whole community of the transgender. You have bravely come out from the shadows, but you still have to face the ignorance that lives in your communities, often behind closed church doors. You are also endangered by the whole evil machinery of hate crimes. Be safe.

12. Climate Change. The political shit storm of semantics. Arguments ensue among politicians who believe that it is not really happening and the ones who at least watch the mega storms, the melting polar caps, and the endangered species and know that man has effectively been ignoring the havoc created by carbon emissions. Anyone who argues that it is some made up political issue raises a lot of suspicion from me. I want to know what companies are funding their campaigns and who they are pandering to when they introduce legislation. Don't you?

Through our unconscionable greed we are poaching endangered animals, losing rain forests, polluting rivers, streams, oceans and drinking water. We are recklessly dependent on coal and its emissions and drilling and fracking for oil like mad scientists obsessed with black gold ignoring the effects on the land and its inhabitants.

What could possibly go wrong?

All of this being said, very powerful people are trying to raise awareness and organizing protests worldwide. Some religious leaders are stepping up to say we are killing the planet. Our former president was not in denial about this crisis. World leaders are taking notice as well. Not so this administration. We are going dangerously backward. You can make a difference. You can write letters to a potential candidate who is running on a platform that is denying climate change and say "Hey, you do not have my vote if you don't support this change." We have a lot of power. Unfortunately, we have a lot of apathy and a lot of misinformation or downright propaganda being spread by clueless media outlets and foreign hackers. No names mentioned. Fake news is also rearing its ugly head as I write.

All environmental agencies, documentaries, politicians, movie stars, athletes, musicians, mega millionaires, religious leaders, film makers, talk shows, blogs and protesters trying to wake up the masses to the reality of the disasters we are creating, you are my heroes!

13. Racism and any form of discrimination. Enslaved goes without saying. We have become a nation of "us and them." Look at the vitriol leveled at the first black president, the fear and distrust leveled at Muslims and refugees. I am ashamed that people are still trying to round up other races and imprison them like the Japanese in WWII or sadly like Hitler. We aren't going to gas them but round them up in camps and then each state can deny them aid. They will be imprisoned and impoverished and abused and denied dignity much like we have done to the African American population for decades and the Native Americans before that. We are also complicit in bombing their countries and then denying them access to escape being killed. We have forgotten Ellis Island and our own roots. I am German, Jewish, Canadian and Scottish. I am not an "us." I am a "them."

A Life Winding Down

I have attended a few gatherings of people and some in my family who have blamed a certain race for all the ills of the world. I am stunned that we have been raised to be elitist assholes based on our skin. I was discreetly raised to believe in the good fortune we had because we were white. We were poor and had no indoor plumbing when I was 5, but, by god, somehow, we were better off due to our light skin. I didn't even buy it then, but often people of my age still say those same backwoods things and the excuse is "I can't help it. I was raised that way." So, we can blame ignorance for our continued racism, but we should all know better.

Moving on to "Christian discrimination." These people use God himself to say we are better than gays, lesbians, transgenders, and of course women. In fact, some even adhere to the concept that a gay person is a sinner and may not go to heaven.

So, we have a racist society, but we pretend that we all have the same rights until we don't.

On the yin and yang side we are now also a society who overwhelmingly believes you should be allowed to marry whomever you please, and to be whatever gender you want to be. Perhaps when all the old racist jerks die off, the young people will kill off racism altogether. That is if social media hasn't tainted their thinking. I am hopeful for the next generation.

To be fully free is to know that we are all connected to one another because we are inhabiting the same planet. To be fully free is to disown racial inequality, gender discrimination, and any form of abuse toward any living thing occupying this same temporary space we have been given.

Barbara Kemm-Highton

To be fully free is to know that time is running out for all of us. To love ourselves and others is the highest form of evolvement we have been offered.

We need to take it.

POEM

I wrote this poem and it has always seemed curious to me about the origin of my thoughts. I was thirty something and still asleep at the wheel. I had little knowledge of a lost civilization that I supposed was just a legend.

Musings

> I have always believed in Atlantis
> Honing my other life at home
> A dishtowel in one hand
> *An American Tragedy* in the other
> I have lived in books and characters
> so mediocrity would not kill me
> with its bare hands.

Any interpretation is left to you. I am baffled by my own musings.

EPILOGUE

When I began this book, I believed that I had so much to absorb. The world changes so fast that we of a certain age are chasing the new information at break-neck speed. I read 5 books at a time and am always amazed that I had never taken the time to know this open-ended puzzle called life. It became overwhelming to watch every documentary and read every new book and to find a new piece to fit. I became almost frantic to complete the massive puzzle in whatever time I have left. The fear of loss of memory or perhaps my early demise would wake me up in the night. I had to leave an important message behind to my loved ones and to make a difference in the world.

But suddenly I knew that it was all a lot simpler. I was awake not asleep anymore.

It is for all of us to simply raise our heads, stop what we are doing, and embrace life. We are only moving about in a body performing tasks like robots. We can at any point realize that we leave these suits we wear behind.

I have no knowledge of what happens after we do ascend or expire or whatever we choose to label the end of our journey, and frankly I believe that might be different for all of us. I do know that pretending that we do not die has postponed our enlightenment and delayed the search for meaning. It is loving and being fully present while we are here that is our only true job. It is about living **knowing** that it is a temporary place.

It is waking up each day with the one mantra that makes any sense. Just for this minute of time, **We Are Fully Here!**

SUGGESTED READING AND OTHER RESOURCES

If you are interested in UFO information, there are many more resources than I will offer, but it will be a place to start. I apologize if I left any author or researcher off the list. Know that all of you are relevant and relentless in your mission to wake us up to the possible secrets of our Universe.

We've Never Been Alone by Paul Von Ward
The Mothman Prophecies by John A. Keel
The Secret History of Extraterrestrials: Advanced Technology and the Coming New Race by Len Kasten
Communion by Whitley Streiber
The Flying Saucers Are Real by Major Donald E. Keyhoe
Missing Time by Bud Hopkins
Our Occulted History: Do the Global Elite Conceal Ancient Aliens by Jim Marrs
Aliens Among Us by Ruth Montgomery

If you prefer television *Ancient Aliens* on the History channel has proven that people are interested. It has had a five year run, 8 seasons and many reruns with an esteemed cast of contributors and narrators: Linda Moulton Howe, an Emmy award winning journalist and expert in cattle mutilations and crop circles for 30 plus years; Nick Pope, a journalist and former employee of the British Ministry of Defense, whose job it was to investigate UFO sightings; Erich Von Däniken, a pioneer in the field, whose book *Chariots of the Gods?* has been read by millions since its publication in 1968, just to name a few. The History Channel and the Destination Channel both are bravely covering all things UFO and paranormal.

I worry about the Internet and like most people I have a love/hate relationship with the sources of information. So

Barbara Kemm-Highton

much of the highway can be contaminated because of the vetting issues related to the authors of the material. That said, it looks like there is a positive response to the information collected, mainly videos, on gaia.com. For a monthly fee you can watch the experts weigh in on the newest information concerning UFOs, extraterrestrials, near death experiences, spirituality and other paranormal subjects.

There are many documentaries that can be found to stream and I recommend *I Know What I Saw,* by award winning film director James Fox. The testimony is impressive because it involves astronauts, military pilots, commercial pilots and government officials. It is available on iTunes.

If you are believer in the government public response that there is no proof that we have had alien contact, then I direct you to the following websites:
www.disclosureproject.org or *www.majesticdocuments.com*

If you are interested in the phenomenon of near death experiences, I lean more toward the earlier reportings that had less of a religious, specifically Christian, message. That is up to you since there seems to be a new one every month in circulation.

Life After Life by Dr. Raymond Moody (author of the term near death experience)
The Light Beyond by Dr. Raymond Moody
Into the Light by Dr. John Lerma (a hospice care doctor)
Learning from the Light by Dr. John Lerma

A BBC documentary on YouTube that has garnered some acclaim is *The Scole Experiment Documentary— Afterlife Investigation.*

The website where the stories of near death experiencers are shared is *nderf.org*

Other authors who have addressed the previous subjects in their books are the late medium Sylvia Brown, the late psychiatrist and expert on death and dying Elizabeth Kubler-Ross, the late seer and healer, Edgar Cayce, the late former

A Life Winding Down

Washington correspondent Ruth Montgomery, and actress and activist, Shirley MacLaine. Any book they have written is compelling.

If you seek spirituality, my "go to" is always the Dalia Lama.

How to Be Compassionate: A handbook for Creating Inner Peace and a Happier World and *A Force for Good* are two good starts.
Soul Lessons and Soul Purpose by Sonia Choquette
Why Healing Happens by O.T. Bonnett M.D.
Heart Thoughts by Louise Hay
The Four Agreements by Don Miguel Ruiz
The Edgar Cayce Primer: Discovering the Path to Self-Transformation by Herbert B Puryear, Ph.D
Miracles by Stuart Wilde

I am afraid that TV itself is woefully lacking in spiritual messages. There are for sure pulpit pounding, pacing, demanding, fear based, theatrical, religious leaders on many channels, but if you are like me, they seem awfully staged and not very relevant, so you must look elsewhere for your dose of spirituality. Oprah's *Super Soul Sunday* is an exception and worth watching.

There are also random non-fiction books that have left a mark on the way I think in many aspects of life and I can only list a few here but perhaps they will keep you thinking about what you believe, too.

Dark Money: The Hidden History of the Billionaires Behind the Rise of the Radical Right by Jane Mayer
Planethood: The Key to Your Future by Benjamin b. Ferencz and Ken Keys Jr.
Dear God What's happening to Us? Halting Eeons of Manipulation by Lynn Grabhorn
The Science of Being Great by Wallace Wattles
Being Mortal by Atul Gawande
Still Foolin' 'Em by Billy Crystal

Barbara Kemm-Highton

The New Rules by Bill Maher
As a Man Thinketh by James Allen
Sage-ing While Age-ing by Shirley MacLaine
The Camino: A Journey of Spirit by Shirley Maclaine

www.ingramcontent.com/pod-product-compliance
Lightning Source LLC
Chambersburg PA
CBHW070117080526
44586CB00013B/1317